Tonight at 10

Kicking Booze
and Breaking News

By Courtney Friel

CONTENTS

PRAISE FOR COURTNEY FRIEL AND *TONIGHT AT 10*

"A raw, honest and unsparing examination of one very famous news anchor's not-so-well-known path to sobriety— Courtney's story will make you laugh, cringe and, ultimately, cheer. Brava!"

—Megyn Kelly, journalist, former Fox News and NBC anchor, and host of *The Kelly File*

"Love Courtney's voice—she's fun, funny, frank and candid! No doubt *Tonight at 10* will help many people struggling with addiction."

—Ben Stein, editorial columnist at *The Wall Street Journal*, host of *Win Ben Stein's Money*

"Addictive, authentic and hilarious."

—Kristen Johnston, actress and star on *3rd Rock from the Sun*

"Raw, powerful, and inspiring...Courtney's experiences with addiction, strength in overcoming it, and hope for a better life are universally relatable. This is a must read for anyone seeking some behind-the-scenes adventures in TV news."

—Jerry O'Connell, actor and TV host

ISBN-13: 978-1-951407-15-5 (paperback)

ISBN-13: 978-1-951407-14-8 (ebook)

This book is dedicated to anyone who thinks their life will suck without alcohol.

INTRODUCTION

#FrielMyVibe: I don't judge. I don't preach. I don't try to convert anyone into living a sober life. It's none of my business what anyone else does with drugs and alcohol. However, I do know what it's like to struggle with addiction, thanks to a very successful 15-year party career. I'm fortunate to have made it to the other side, having not had a sip of booze, a drug or a mind-altering substance for over a decade, ever since 09/09/09. Trust me, I was never planning on having this journey—but the experience ended up giving me a life beyond my wildest dreams. Cheesy as that may sound, I do feel like I've stumbled upon an awesome secret, and now is the right time to share it with you.

As a "put-together" news anchor, most people would never guess that I'm in recovery. Allow me to remind you that substance abuse does not discriminate. It affects every single demographic and all walks of life. According to the latest statistics, an estimated 47.7 million Americans struggle with substance abuse, and the opioid crisis is currently dominating the national discussion. Lives are destroyed every day. In the time I was writing this book alone, two people I knew personally died from accidentally overdosing: my good friend's husband who was a fireman and my co-worker, KTLA anchor Chris Burrous. Both left behind young children they adored.

I didn't publicly share about my sobriety until I was clean for six years. I figured that was enough time to at least be credible on the matter. However, once I did finally go public on social media, posting tidbits about being sober on Instagram, the flood gates opened. People ask me daily how I got (and continue to be) drug and alcohol free. They like my vulnerability. Viewers message me about how my posts helped them quit drinking and smoking pot, or encouraged them to get back on the wagon. And then there are those who are surprised or can't understand why I came out of the closet given my public TV persona.

Here's the deal: we live in a tell-all culture, but there's still a taboo around addiction and sobriety. No one gets a rainbow or a parade for coming out. Most people hold their sobriety cards close to the vest, even those who publicly advocate the virtues of authenticity and owning your truth. I recently inspired one of those self-help women to "come out" and post about her 20-year sober anniversary to her followers on social media. The feedback she received was incredibly supportive. I've also had a bunch of news anchors and reporters from around the country write that my openness gave them the courage to share their sober milestones with their viewers.

I firmly believe that sobriety is cool and should be celebrated. I'm also a firm believer in the power of sharing and am not ashamed that my brain is wired differently. It doesn't allow me to have just a single drink; I want to keep going, find some cocaine and be up until the birds are chirping. The truth was, I just wasn't a fan of feeling feelings. If I could numb them out, I did.

Fortunately, through a lot of work, prayer, self-control and a huge commitment to meditation, I learned to live a sober (and fun!) life without numbing out. Facing my fears and problems head-on, with clarity and focus, has made me a much stronger person. That's why I feel a calling and deep sense of purpose to help people in their sobriety journey. It's my soul intention for writing this book. I'm not here to tell you what to do. All I can do is Keep it Friel, and share what worked for me (and what didn't).

.

CHAPTER 1
BIG HOT MESS

*"You can't keep dancing with the devil and ask
why you're still in hell."*
—*Kynna Claire*

By the time I was 21 years old, and given the asshole I'd become, I thought having liver damage from drinking was an amazing accomplishment—and that's not counting my other organ destruction from doing massive amounts of cocaine and downers. At the time, I was pursuing a career as a prime-time TV news anchor and a serious party girl. It's a small miracle that I didn't end up like Heath Ledger, whose death I covered on TV while hanging onto my own wasted wits by a thin thread.

When you're fucked up all the time but still manage, like I did, to hold down a job (miraculously, I've gotta say), you do stupid, dangerous shit. For example: I downed 19 shots of vodka on my 19th birthday. I drank so much one night with an old high-school crush that I blacked out and woke up the next morning in his upstairs hallway, buck-naked, with my thong by my side, his cat on my head, and his father looking down on me in disbelief (to this day, one of the most embarrassing moments of my life).

Raging all night at hot clubs also became a passion, along with crossing the California border into Tijuana to buy colorful pottery, fake designer purses, duty-free alcohol and muscle relaxers at local pharmacies. On another occasion, I drove across the border and did lines with a friend in broad daylight. A Mexican police officer, or *federale*, spotted us and said it would cost $200 not to get in trouble. I gave him the cash and had the balls to ask him if he could give the blow back. (Lo and behold, he did! I later went to a party in San Diego with it and told everyone there: "Y'all, the blow tonight was *really* expensive!)

I was still able to put on a pretty TV face and report on-camera to millions of Americans, though my escalating substance abuse was slowly starting to seep through the cracks. After a long day hosting Season Four of *World Poker Tour* in Las Vegas, I ended up eating and drinking with the crew until 4 am, then passed out *in* my plate of spaghetti with my strappy red dress falling off. The creator of the show called my agent the next day and asked: "Uh, do we have a problem here?" *Ya think?*

I was 15 years old the first time I got drunk. I drank too many beers way too fast, then came home and threw up in the shower. My mom found the puke towel the next day and grounded me. Still, I loved the way I felt when I was buzzed: pain-free and fun-loving. Instead of Shy Courtney (yes, I *was* shy; more on that shortly), Reporter Friel came out. I'd whip out my Zima bottle filled with Jolly Ranchers and turn it into a microphone to conduct interviews with anyone who crossed my path. The fact that my high school had a well-equipped TV production studio was a big bonus. It soon became my home away from home.

I worked in the school TV studio every day until 10 pm at night with a "work hard, play hard" mentality. I created my own show, anchored morning announcements, reported on teacher strikes, interviewed local congressmen, covered sports games, and profiled exchange students. In my junior year, I sent an audition tape to Channel One's *Student Produced Week*, a now-defunct news show that, back then, was like *The Mickey Mouse Club* for journalists. Anderson Cooper, Maria Menounos and Lisa Ling, among others, all started there. It was hugely popular—half of the middle and high schools in the country were contracted to air the channel in their classrooms. Once a year, they'd fly 20 students from all over the country out to Los Angeles for two weeks to put on the show. There were seven anchor positions available the year I sent in my tape. To my incredible joy, I was chosen for one of them.

I fell in love not just with Los Angeles but with the TV business as well. This major dream-come-true, however, simply added fuel to a fire that was already raging. I had been the target of relentless bullying for years throughout my youth, which in turn fed my substance abuse and increasingly reckless behavior.

Let me back up and say that I was the least likely person to engage in any kind of bad behavior when I was growing up. I was raised in the small town of Audubon, Pennsylvania —the home of birdwatching! Someone once told me that Pennsylvania has the highest ratio of people who never leave the 50-mile radius of where they were born. I have no idea if that's true, but I repeat it like it is because that was definitely the case in my town. Perhaps that's why so many of my high school friends married each other, and why their parents and grandparents did the same—there was nothing better to do!

One of the things I *did* do a lot back then was watch the news with my dad, specifically the local ABC station in Philly followed by *World News Tonight* with Peter Jennings. I adored Peter Jennings. He was the gold standard of TV journalism: stoic, confident, and comforting. I bawled my eyes out the day he died (still the only celebrity death I've ever cried about). By the third grade I knew that I wanted to work in television news, but in order to do so I had one important milestone to cross: I had to get over my pathological shyness.

People who know me now would never believe I was ever shy (though most would never believe I was an addict, either). People say I have no filter and would probably even call me "Miss TMI" behind my back. I'm often judged as snobby or stuck-up, probably because I look like the self-proclaimed #NewsBarbie you see on camera. I got Fox-ified when I started working at Fox News Channel, with a $5,000 per year clothing allowance and tons of designer dresses at cost. At KTLA, which I call the Fox News of local news, my bosses want the women anchors to have big hair, wear tons of makeup and fake eyelashes and look seriously glam, even if we're reporting on a murder in Compton. But even if I may seem like a pageant girl, I'm actually very down-home. Two of my favorite places to shop are 99-cent stores and Ross Dress for Less—and I can talk to anyone about anything.

For many years, however, I was intensely shy and relentlessly bullied. They say that life imitates art, but in my case, my life imitated my first-ever TV commercial gig. I was 15 years old when I went on the audition. It was for Love's Baby Soft, a perfume that The Awl blog once described as "the most feminine of all feminine products to have ever existed on Earth," one that "smells like babies." I didn't even have a headshot back then, but I got the main role as the Love's Baby Soft girl anyhow (and got paid a whopping $300 for it). In that commercial, a group of high school students eye each other in a classroom as a voice-over explains who's got a crush on who: *"Cathy likes Jack. Jack, however, has his eye on Beth...which is too bad, because Beth is dating Scott. Which isn't too cool with Beth's friend Heather, because Scott used to be her boyfriend..."*

The girls scowl at each other until the voice-over stops and the teacher asks the class to welcome a new student. With that, I walk into the room and smile at everyone: the pretty, blonde new face of Love's Baby Soft. All eyes turn to me. The boys go gaga. The girls get pissed. And I'm immediately a target.

That pretty much described my real life growing up: I was bullied and taunted. It started around age six on a playdate. The two girls I was playing with ganged up on me for no reason, and I called my mom crying to pick me up. In seventh grade, I was stuck at a lunch table where the girls told me they didn't like me and that I was ugly. At a pep rally in the gymnasium, an entire section of kids once repeatedly shouted: *"We hate Courtney Friel!"*

Then there was the day my classmates all made spirit bags for one another. Whoever picked the paper with my name on it had apparently chosen to rip it up, since I was the only person who didn't get a decorated bag with candy in it. In high school, most of the culprits were mean girls whose queen I called Bitcherelli. She was tall and skinny, mousy with brown frizzy hair, and sported a fuzzy girl-mustache. People kissed her ass because she was the captain of the field hockey and lacrosse teams. I'm pretty sure they were all terrified of her.

Bitcherelli came into my world with a shank. I was standing around at lacrosse practice minding my own business when out of nowhere, she pulled down my green Umbro shorts in front of everyone. I looked back at her with a *why-the-fuck-would-you-do-that* expression on my face. "Sorry!" she yelled back with a smirk—and that was the beginning.

Bitcherelli and her posse of mean girls continued to bully me for years. They'd stalk me in hallways, accuse me of talking shit about people I didn't know and threaten to beat me up in fistfights. Their catty comments about my appearance escalated into comments about what a slut and whore I was—which was ironic considering I graduated high school a virgin, unlike all my girlfriends (who lost their v-cards at age 14).

As a newly-minted hooker-virgin, I tried to ignore the abuse and kept a smile on my face to diffuse the aggression. That categorically did not work. One day, my car door got keyed and the word SLUT was written in big black letters across my windshield by a guy who was pissed off that I wouldn't hook up with him. I frantically tried to wipe the slur off and failed—it had been written in permanent marker. I drove away in tears, looking past the awful word all the way back to my house (which had recently been egged and toilet-papered). Nothing was done after my mom reported the incident to my school; the perpetrator was the high school football team's star player, and the assistant principal was the head football coach. You get the picture.

Bitcherelli and her posse continued to harass me and the guy who keyed my car started a ridiculous rumor that I'd sucked a host's dick while I was in LA for *Student Produced Week*. I continued to find solace in booze, my trusted companion.

In many ways, I can thank those teen tormenters for helping me grow thicker skin, which is an essential feature for any serious anchor in the TV business. As I later learned, there will always be haters who love to dissect you to pieces —and yes, I do get letters and emails from bullies who feel a burning desire to criticize me or tell me, like one jackass did, that my knees look like pig snouts! Dude, we can't all have Heidi Klum and Gisele Bündchen knees, okay?!

Over time, I decided that success would be my best revenge.

Since high school, I've covered stories about horrible school shootings by psychopaths who were bullied in their youth, or cowardly bullies who inflicted mental torment on others via the internet, anonymously sowing seeds of hate. I now know that bullying is an expression of deep-seated childhood pain, which is why I advise people not only to confront bullies, but to kill them with kindness. I learned personally—the hard way—that bullies need to be confronted, not ignored. But that wisdom came later.

In my teens, I was basically clueless. I refused to stoop down to the same level as my bullies. I chose to turn the other cheek, an approach I can chalk up to years of going to Presbyterian church every Sunday until I was 18. But I also didn't have the courage to stand up for myself, and ignoring those bullies only empowered them even more. I tried to act nonchalant, but on the inside, I was stuffing my emotional pain into a tiny box, where it festered. I felt like I didn't belong. I begged my parents to send me to private school, but they took me to church counseling instead, where all I got were unhelpful tips about retorting with snarky remarks or not taking things personally.

Fortunately, everything was about to get much easier—thanks to alcohol. Bottoms up!

> "At first, addiction is maintained by pleasure. But the intensity of this pleasure gradually diminishes and the addiction is then maintained by avoidance of pain."
> —Frank Tallis

My two careers—budding TV news journalist and raging party girl—really took off when I was done with high school and was lucky enough to attend the excellent TV journalism program at Elon University in North Carolina. I became the host of *Elon Today* and began my hardcore professional training as a news anchor. My hardcore training as a High Priestess of Partying had also begun. At Elon, I'd drink every night until 2 am and come up with all sorts of reasons to imbibe. "Come on ladies, it's the new moon!" I'd enthuse to my girlfriends. "That's what we're celebrating tonight!"

By that time, I no longer drank to numb out emotional

pain; I simply loved getting fucked up! And I could not stop at one drink. I wanted to keep going until the sun came up because frankly, why waste the calories if you're not getting a buzz? Back in the day, I wasn't a fan of feelings (or "Frielings," as I call them). If I could numb them out, all the better. I was having a blast, even if I was puking in my loft bed or dry-heaving in the shower every morning before class. Eventually I started rolling on Ecstasy, the synthetic drug also known as MDMA that the kids now call "Molly." Part stimulant and part hallucinogen, Ecstasy gave me the happiest and warmest feelings in the world—that is, until they started to wear off.

I wasn't aware that by adding pills to my alcohol repertoire, I'd be rounding a bend—I mean, I wasn't hurting anyone other than myself, right? When talking about his own road to recovery, author Augusten Burroughs wrote: "I would never drink cologne and am therefore not an alcoholic." In so many words, I, like Burroughs, wasn't drinking cologne either. Ergo, I wasn't an alcoholic. Talk about denial.

In fact, let's talk about *denial* for a second. Denial is one of the most common symptoms of alcoholism. An article in the Very Well Mind blog identifies the following seven symptoms of alcohol denial:

1. *Rationalization:* "Hey, everyone else in my life is doing it, including many of my colleagues. I still go to work and look like I have my shit together (husband, job, make-up, clothes). What's the big deal?"
2. **Dismissing:** See above.
3. *Blame:* "Booze isn't illegal, and most of the pills I take are prescribed by doctors. Plus, my job is super-stressful, so I need something to calm my anxiety and help me sleep or I won't even be able to do my work! And if I can't do my work, how will I survive?"

4. **Concealing:** It feels cool to do cocaine and Ecstasy and keep it a secret. Go figure.
5. **Making Comparisons:** See 1.
6. **False Agreements:** See 3.
7. *Defensiveness: "Why are you even asking? What's your problem?"*

The bottom line? I had all seven symptoms of denial but was in too deep to recognize them! (But more on that rabbit hole in Chapter Three.)

I finally lost my v-card in a college frat house. I'd held onto my virginity for the first two months of college, but after so many nightly sleepovers with my then-boyfriend, I caved in on Valentine's Day night and had sex with him…for all of 20 seconds. We did it again the next night for another 20 seconds, and then the two-pump-chump broke up with me because he said I was an alcoholic. Who, *me*? *An alcoholic*?

I was absolutely crushed. My friends were mad at me for giving it up to him, but hey, at least I'd set the sex bar low. Desperate to numb out the break-up pain, I went on a bender for the rest of the school year. On my 19th birthday, after downing 19 shots of vodka throughout the day, I went to Miami with my girlfriends for spring break, cut my hair super short, bleached it blonde and got my tongue pierced (which looked *real* classy on college news).

I soon added cocaine to my bag of goodies and instantly hooked. I tricked an older high school friend into giving me some when I was home on a break; to get it, I lied and said I'd done it before. I woke up the next morning in my childhood bedroom with a nosebleed. My friend at Elon, Erika, had also tried coke during the break, and we both loved the experience! The first time we were able to get some at Elon, we ran around the football field in the middle of the night shouting about how it was the greatest drug ever. Erika and I then did anything we could to score it, including making out with each other in front of guys as a bartering chip.

Our first experience involved a guy named Anthony and an entire bottle of tequila. With some cheesy porno playing in the background, the three of us jumped in the shower and then poured chocolate and strawberry sauce on each other in bed. I guess it was amateur hour because there was no sex or penetration involved in this so-called threesome. We were there for the coke, remember?

After tiring of all the sorority snobs at Elon, working on every TV show the school had and stealing all of my room-mate's Ritalin, I decided to move to Los Angeles. Erika came along for the ride. I'd soon learn that people in the City of Angels were way too into themselves to care just how chroni-cally wasted I was about to become.

> "Hollywood is wonderful. Anyone who doesn't like it is
> either crazy or sober."
> — Raymond Chandler

Erika and I moved into an apartment on the Westside of Los Angeles. We were ambitious blonde party girls with fake IDs and zero cleaning skills. We'd bring grocery carts into the apartment from the street and fill them up with dirty laundry and trash. We both got jobs at a nearby tanning salon where our boss, a short man with black eyes and long curly hair (who oddly looked just like my Cavalier King Charles Spaniel named Stoli), provided us with copious amounts of free cocaine. We'd drink and snort lines with him in the back room until the sun came up. In no time, we were skinny tan cokeheads who lived in filth.

By the end of that school year, my daily coke habit had started to take its toll—even if it *was* the only year of college I got straight As. I would leave my classes and library study sessions at Santa Monica College to do blow in the bathrooms to jack up my energy and focus. Looking back now, it's clear that I was a much better learner, listener and communicator when I was *off* all the chemicals—but I didn't know that at the time.

I was having frequent panic attacks that felt like there was a man standing on my chest. One night, my anxiety got so severe that I thought I was having a heart attack and drove myself to the emergency room. My EKG and CT scan checked out fine; it turned out I was just suffering from massive heartburn from all the shitty vodka and diet soda I'd been drinking. More serious long-term physical ailments were brewing, however—ailments that would plague me long after I got sober (but more on that in Chapter Nine.)

I decided to transfer to San Diego State University for my junior year. I was done living with Erika. She was stealing my underwear and my Vicodin, and she'd even tried to hook up with my boyfriend. As soon as I got there, I began having daily headaches that lasted for three straight years. I became famous in SDSU's infirmary for needing weekly Demerol and Toradol shots in my butt cheeks (which gradually gave way to gigantic bruises). I tried everything under the sun to get rid of the headaches, including every possible migraine medicine available. I did food and stress diaries but couldn't find any common triggers. I got an MRI. I tried acupuncture and every holistic headache contraption you can imagine. Two neurologists eventually gave up on me. It was during that period of fruitless testing that a doctor told me about my liver damage from drinking, and I had the gall to think it was a milestone (the kind you celebrate, that is).

After getting that news, I did quit booze one month — which was really hard considering my job at the time was as a liquor promoter, the perfect gig for an alcoholic. I got paid $25 an hour to hang out at a bar in a slutty outfit and hand out free shots and swag.

I moved out to live at the beach and soon became a peculiar guest at house parties there. Coked up with chest pain, I'd rummage through freezers for frozen bags of peas or ice packs to put over my heart. When people would ask me what was wrong, I'd cheerfully explain that I thought I was having a heart attack—and would then do another line. I also peer-pressured other people to "go skiing" and try a bump with me. I even got my college boyfriend hooked. (Years later, he developed a serious addiction, though he has since gone to rehab and is sober today).

I was still as ambitious as ever despite my escalating substance abuse. I'd landed a correspondent gig on Oprah's channel, Oxygen, and also completed internships at MTV News and KNSD, an NBC affiliate station in San Diego, before graduating from SDSU in 2002 with a degree in political science. I'd come a long way from being a skinny tan cokehead who lived in filth. I was now a normal-sized, somewhat-paler coke-head who would soon be entering the "real world" of broadcast news.

Love's Baby soft girl, 16 years old

Passed out with my plastic vodka bottle

CHAPTER 2
TRAIN WRECK

"Nothing can make me feel better now, except for cocaine."
—*Dylan Moran*

My first anchor-slash-reporter job was at WBBJ, the ABC affiliate in Jackson, Tennessee. The station was located in the middle of Tennessee's Bible Belt, housed in a pale pink Quonset hut with corrugated sheet metal walls like the ones you'd see in a Kuwaiti war zone. Ironically, it was also in the middle of a park that was a gay hangout—a place where men in bright, sleeveless crop tops lingered by their cars waiting to have sex with one another. Hence, my nickname for WBBJ: *WB-Blowjob in Jack-off, Tennessee.*

I packed up my Mazda and drove across the country to take the gig, one that paid an illustrious salary of $18,000 per year. I was 23 years old and soon became the main primetime anchor at the only news station in town. Looking back, I had no business being there—but hey, that's how we all start out in the biz. On my first day on the job, I was woken up by the sound of baseball-sized hailstones pounding on the roof. Heavy wind was shaking the walls of the building and warning sirens were blaring. Scared shitless, I walked outside into the turbulence of an F4 tornado—the first in a series of tornadoes that would blast their way across multiple states to become the most severe tornado outbreak sequence in recorded history.

The hail smashed my car's windows, pockmarked its entire body and flooded the interior with water. It was totaled in an instant. A news photographer picked me up in the live truck and we headed downtown after the first tornado wreaked its havoc. The city had been transformed into a war zone: toppled trees, downed power lines and crushed cars were littered over the concrete. Dwellings were blown to smithereens. I trudged through piles of random debris that had been violently thrown together. For some reason, I remember a Bible, a hacksaw and a Barbie doll.

We filmed on location in a demolished school and at a Pringles factory where literally thousands of sour cream and onion cans were strewn everywhere—and spoke with dazed and injured residents. But the worst sight ever, by far, was a trailer park where dead babies were found in trees, hurled there by cyclonic winds. At least 42 deaths were reported across five states along with hundreds of injuries and millions of dollars of damage.

The wrath of Mother Nature and the devastation I saw that first week on the job was just the beginning of the horrible shit I would see in my line of work: mass shootings, wildfires, plane crashes, sexual assaults, home invasions, child abuse, gang murders and hit-and-runs (which abound in LA, the hit-and-run capital of the world). And that's just the "ordinary" stuff.

I've also covered transients giving birth in toilets, a man hoarding 400 dead snakes in his house, and cross-dressing thieves. Then there was stuff so twisted it would drive anyone to the bottle.

There was the eight-year-old boy who was brutally

tortured and beaten to death by his mother and her boyfriend. Their heinous acts included shooting him with a BB gun, burning him, cutting him, forcing him to eat kitty litter and locking him in a box. I had to stare at photos of his dead body for several days in court. And then there was the guy who murdered his fiancée by scalping and mutilating her body. I had to look at gruesome evidence pictures of *that* case, too—pictures of her scalped head, scalp pieces, and her ear were laid out on table. There was also the Riverside couple who starved, tortured and chained their 13 kids to their beds.

All that doesn't include the aftermath of freak car accidents I had to witness. There were white sheets draped over dead bodies and other gruesome sights, like the brain of a 17-year-old boy being picked off the wheel of the Mack Truck that hit him. It never gets easier seeing family members show up at the scene of a car accident, either. Two of the worst cases were the man who watched his entire family burn alive in a minivan because he couldn't get them out in time before it exploded, and the parents who lost their only daughter after two guys racing on the freeway caused an accident, one that left four high schoolers who were driving home from Disneyland decapitated. I sobbed along with the mom and dad. I just couldn't help it.

Believe it or not, this is par-for-the-course when it comes to local news. I call it *"death du jour."* I often feel like an obituary reporter: if it bleeds, it leads. Before I got sober, I'd chase away the ghosts of these gruesome moments with booze or coke. That first WBBJ job was doubly challenging because I did the job of 10 people: anchor, reporter, photographer, editor, producer, writer, teleprompter roller, hair, makeup and news van driver. But it was all worthwhile when, at 11 pm, I'd end my shift with my nightly ritual: hot wings and vodka sodas with lemon. I'd slam down as many as I could drink before closing time and stumble back to my apartment down the street. Every. Damn. Night.

I didn't have to be at work until 2 pm the next day and couldn't find any cocaine in such a small town (except for the one time I made out with my manicurist for a gram), so what was the problem? It didn't dawn on me until years later that the tornado I'd covered that first day on the job was a metaphor for my life at that time: a train wreck in the making.

"You're not drunk if you can lie on the floor without holding on."
—*Dean Martin*

In 2002, I met my husband-to-be, Carter Evans, in San Diego at an NBC internship. I'd had a major crush on Carter watching him report the news on NBC, admiring his story-telling, good looks, confidence and playfulness. He eventually became an extremely helpful mentor to me, and we dated long-distance throughout my time in Tennessee. A year later, I accepted his marriage proposal and moved back to Los Angeles, where he'd started working at CBS. My WBBJ news director told me I would fall on my face if I tried to work in LA. *Yeah, maybe if I'm drunk enough*, I thought.

The wedding preparations happened slowly, but sadly, I was already married to alcohol and coke. What should have been the happiest time of my life turned out to be filled with drama. I binged on blow for the two weeks leading up to the wedding. When my drug dealer randomly showed up at my apartment, I remember thinking that was concerning. I'm convinced he gave me coke laced with meth that night, because I felt extra speedy and ended up in front of the mirror picking at my skin. I saw zits popping up all over my face and body. Who knows if they were really there, but I woke up the next day with horrible scabs, feeling extra ashamed, depressed, and in need of long sleeves and a bucket of cover-up. Another go-to self-mutilation technique I'd turn to when high on coke was using a dental pick, designed for scraping tartar off your teeth, to dig out my gums until my mouth was full of blood. *Who does that?* Drug addicts!

I drank shots of vodka before meeting with the pastor who was marrying us. After the rehearsal dinner, I made out with one of my girlfriends and her husband got so mad he slammed me up against a wall in a chokehold. I then woke my parents up in their hotel room, crying about the incident. After downing 22 drinks throughout the big day (which I barely recall), I ended up getting in a blowout fight with my brand-new husband, dancing on a bar, then somehow losing the bottom part of my dress and my sparkly shoes—and I never found them either!

We didn't even have sex on our wedding night! Aside from being incredibly annoying while drunk, I also had the tendency to become stubborn and pick fights about anything. Carter was understandably extremely upset, but that didn't stop the train wreck from happening.

For the next few years, I got host and correspondent gigs on E! News, Court TV, Travel Channel, Fox's *America's Most Wanted*, and anchored mini newscasts that people could watch on their cell phones. At one point I had six different jobs and worked 25 days in a row. I would even drive out to Palm Springs—two hours each way—to freelance report and anchor at the CBS station there because I missed local news.

One night, I had to edit my story back at the station, so I stopped at a drive-through for a bite before heading to the gas station to pick up a large beer. I emptied out my soda, poured the beer into the cup and secretly drank it while I was in the editing bay. I had a pretty little clear and purple "bumper" that I would take snorts of blow from, too. My drug use often made the drives to and from the desert difficult—I was either too tired or too speedy. One time, I'd taken a tad too much Ephedra, which had already been banned by the FDA, and started having a panic attack. I threw the pills out the window after making a pact with God that I would never take them again. Another time, I was so tired driving back at midnight that I pulled off the freeway and into a parking lot. I had to pee really bad, and when I saw there weren't any restaurants open, I literally peed in the backseat of my car before napping. Not my proudest moment.

My substance abuse hit new highs when I moved to New York City in February 2007 and was hired to be the face of foxnews.com. At the time, I was the youngest person to be hired for an on-air position at the channel at just 26 years old. I thought I'd have a gradual buildup of TV time, but instead I was thrust onto all the shows at once. I even hosted *Fox & Friends* my very first weekend there! I was completely unprepared for it and felt totally uncomfortable. My only saving grace was that Britney Spears had shaved her head the night before, so I had a pop culture story to speak on.

Once again, I found myself the target for bullies—except this time they were primarily online. Blogs called me the "bikini bonehead anchor" after someone dug up pictures I'd done for Maxim and FHM from a *World Poker Tour* shoot. They would write that I was "pretty, but an idiot," and that I didn't deserve all the airtime I was getting. Internally, the rumor about me was that I'd gotten the job because I already knew one of the bosses from meeting him in Wildwood, New Jersey and that maybe he wanted to sleep with me— but Wildwood, New Jersey was a place I'd never even been to! In reality, my agent had sent Fox News Corporation my news reels.

Just like I'd done with my high school bullies, I internalized all the hurtful comments—but relief was always only a bar away. I'd drink after hours with coworkers and turn into that annoying girl on the hunt for cocaine. I'll keep my famous party pals' identities a secret, but here's one hint: I did lines in one anchor's closet before he came out of the closet! I also had a handful of random dealers who would show up wherever I was to give me a gram of blow in a small plastic bag or a vial for $60—or an eight-ball for $180. I'd often invite them to party with me.

Anyone who tries to romanticize cocaine needs to remember this: most cokeheads don't sit in big mansions by a fireplace on white shag carpets and snort pristine powder off fancy mirrored tables (although I did do that once). More often than not, they do bumps off the back of a dirty toilet in a nasty bathroom filled with messages like "Larry sucks mad dick" scribbled on the stalls. They stay up all night and get depressed when the coke runs out, as the sun rises and birds chirp. They wake up starving in the late afternoon and scarf down an entire take-out pizza, feeling like shit about themselves—and then they start up again the next day. That, more or less, was me. It was a vicious cycle. Each time I'd wake up feeling like shit, I'd immediately go into self-hatred mode. Then I would set rules (which I'd never follow) such as only drinking on the weekends, or only drinking one night during the work week.

While I was the newsreader on *Fox & Friends Weekend*, I was primarily concerned about making sure my cocaine was lined up before I went out drinking; then I'd hit brunch spots when the morning show ended, drink bottomless mimosas, pass out and miss the whole day. I once puked in the kitchen of a popular restaurant and got kicked out. I also barfed right in the middle of Eighth Avenue in front of a bunch of people.

I had some close calls on those weekend mornings, struggling through hangovers. I once partied until 2 am and had to be up at 4 am for the first 6 am news cut-in—clearly not enough time to sleep off the drugs and booze. I was still wasted and tried to chug as much water as I could while getting my makeup done. On camera under bright lights at the news desk that morning with my heart pounding hard, I once again prayed to God to get through the next two minutes without becoming a YouTube moment. When the camera started to roll, I put on a smile and said: "From Americassss Newzzzzroom...I'm Courtnayyy Frieeel." I swore to myself I would never cut it that close again.

Thankfully I never got in trouble with my bosses, although they knew about my party girl reputation. Clearly, they thought I had poor judgment and was a loose cannon. Say what you want about Fox News, but they were super gracious when I decided to get help (though more details on that in Chapter Three). But even that close call didn't stop me from putting on the brakes. And my pill problem was picking up speed too.

I always needed Xanax to bring me down from coke, but I also kept a bottle on me at all times in case I got stuck underground in the subway and had a panic attack. A shrink had given me Adderall to help me stay focused, so I would get up really early, pop a pill, then look for story ideas while I worked out on my mini-elliptical. I'd snort it if I needed a bigger boost, which allowed me to drink a lot more too. At the end of the day, sleeping pills helped me go to bed early enough so I could get up for the morning show the next day. (While I'm on the subject, I'll note this: doctors in New York write prescriptions for pills like they're candy. Lots of them take cash since many don't take insurance, so they give you what you want to keep you coming back —get it?)

Ambien was the beginning of the end. I loved the high I got when I fought off sleep, and having sex on it was off the chain (or so I thought until I got sober and realized that, hey, sex is so much better when you're not fucked up). Loopy from Ambien, I'd bargain-shop online in a daze. Later, random things I had no recollection of ordering would show up on my doorstep—jewelry, clothes, shoes. I'd also wake up to crazy Facebook messages I'd posted with no memory of having written them. Around this time, I also thought it was a great idea to incorporate Ambien into my partying, which made me black-out more frequently.

With my brain scrambled from uppers and downers, I felt like shit all the time and didn't like the person I was becoming. I was supposed to be Murphy Brown, but I was looking more like Anna Nicole Smith (the skinny version). I even stole pills from my husband's supply...and from his mother and grand-mother's medicine cabinets when we'd visit them. For the first time, I was starting to worry about either getting busted buying coke from a shady dealer and losing my job or dying in my sleep like any number of recent celebrities: Heath Ledger from an accidental overdose of prescription pills, DJ AM the following year after mixing cocaine, Oxycodone and Lorazepam, take your pick. That could have easily been my fate—there was one night I had Ecstasy, alcohol, coke, pot, Xanax and muscle relaxers in my system. I should have died!

Sometimes you have to romance death before you stop playing with fire. Or you have to see yourself as a raving moron before you get a grip on yourself—you have to have what I call your "David Hasselhoff hamburger moment" (if you're too young to know what that is, please use the Google). Here's one of mine:

I was on an evening train heading back into New York City after partying all day in the Hamptons. I already had copious amounts of alcohol and cocaine in my system when I decided to pop some Ambien and Xanax to get another high. There I was: 29 years old, married, and a news anchor and correspondent at Fox News Channel. Carter was sitting someplace else on the train. For some reason, I took off my padded strapless bra, tied it around my head, and pretended it was a crown I'd just won at a beauty pageant. My friend Ann filmed me with her cell phone, asking me questions about winning the "Miss 34-C Cup Queen" title (which, by the way, was really a B-cup). I grabbed some random guy standing next to me, pretended he was my boyfriend and asked him if he was proud that I won the crown. I was certain that the people sitting around us thought I was hysterical—and that they might even recognize me from TV! I went home and passed out, as usual.

About a week later, Ann emailed me the video of our train antics. I had no recollection of it at all. I watched it in my Fox News office, absolutely stunned and horrified. I was beyond wasted. My eyes were barely open and I was slurring, snorting and flopping all over the place. In my hair were chunks of blueberry pie, which had gotten there after I'd smashed said pie in my face at the party earlier. My impromptu BF and his pals were not amused; in fact, they looked disgusted. Seeing myself in this state was a huge wake-up call—or so I thought. Apparently, I needed one more push into the deep end.

Shortly thereafter, on Labor Day weekend, I was with three other couples at my parents' vacation house in Florida. At this point, Carter was aware that I was abusing Ambien. He'd already confronted me on the issue multiple times and had thrown my pills away. I'd agreed to stop taking them, but he still had his own supply (for his crazy morning hours working at CNN). The first day in Florida, our group went absolutely bonkers on alcohol overload. A few of the guys went to a thrift store, bought two baby strollers, and filled them up with beer to take to the beach. Later that day, the strollers ended up in my parents' pool.

It was pouring outside. Our loud conversations and laughter were irritating the neighbors. More drama ensued that resulted in yelling, splashing and crying. I went to my bedroom and took a big handful of pills to numb everything out. Though I wasn't trying to kill myself, I did end up passed out on the living room floor. My friends couldn't wake me up but they somehow managed to get me into bed. When I woke up the next morning, head throbbing and about to puke, Carter told me that I needed to go to inpatient rehab or he'd divorce me. If I didn't yell back "fuck you" at the time, I was definitely thinking it. He went downstairs and came back up with the three other couples. Everyone surrounded my bed and looked down at me. Still semi-blasted, I looked up at their faces and thought: *Shit, is this an intervention?*

Miss 34-C queen on the LIRR train

Bad hangover while cleaning up after an epic BBQ

CHAPTER 3
REHAB MAKEOVER

"Man, I really wish I didn't get sober."
—Nobody ever

Dear Vodka: When we first met, you made me feel on top of the world. Holding you in my apple martini glass, I felt funny, confident, popular and glamorous. But your side-effects— throwing up, blacking out, passing out, slurring, gossiping, arguing, being hungover—made me feel just the opposite, and happened far too frequently.

I embarrassed myself so much that I earned the titles hot mess, lush, sloppy drunk and party girl, and I definitely compromised my values. You were so predictable though. I needed one more thing every time we drank...

Cocaine: At first you helped me get skinny and good grades. I felt like I was part of a secret club, a badass, or a celebrity—especially when I was doing lines with actual celebrities. But it wasn't all big mirrored tables and long piles of white snow. It was more like bathroom stalls and long nights of racing heartbeat, panic, self-injury, and oh, the depression after! You ruined my wedding. I hate how addictive you are.

Bottom line: You've both made my life unmanageable and out of *control. FU. We're done. It's over. Cut out. I'm so much better without you.*

That was the note I wrote to my addiction in rehab. Yup, I'd decided to say yes to the seven people who'd surrounded my bed and convinced me to get help at an inpatient treatment facility. Even with a gnarly hangover, I'd thankfully had enough functional brain cells in those crucial moments to realize I deserved more for my life and had more to offer this world. It ended up being the best decision I'd ever made.

My husband called and explained the situation to my agent, who then dealt with my bosses at Fox News, telling them where I would be for at least the next 28 days. Top brass was very understanding and grateful I was being proactive about my problem rather than giving them some sort of public scandal to clean up instead.

Of the 14,000 treatment centers in the US, I wanted to choose one that would let me stay close to New York City to miss as little work as possible, but I also needed someplace in-network to be covered by insurance. Several phone calls later and viola, Silver Hill in New Canaan, Connecticut had a bed waiting for me. I was still dazed and shocked by this journey I was about to embark on, and I didn't feel like drinking. But I knew I had to have one last cocktail, right? I remember thinking: "*This is such a shitty last drink.*" But with limited options, I imbibed a raspberry vodka and 7-Up like a champ and popped some Adderall just for kicks. I flew back from Florida, packed my bags, and hopped on a train to Connecticut.

I arrived at Silver Hill on September 8th, 2009. I was scared to death and felt so raw, icky, vulnerable and shameful. During check-in, I was given a cup to pee in and got a full-body search (inside some crevices too, I think). All of my belongings were searched as well. My blackberry (aka my "crackberry") was to be taken away for the entire stay! The registration lady told me my sobriety date would be the following day. She wrote it down on a piece of paper: 09/09/09. I later learned that some people plan their sober dates, but the numerical alignment of this one was pure coincidence—and a pretty rad reason to not want to fuck it up!

Silver Hill's campus was absolutely beautiful. I had picked the right time to go (again unintentionally) as it was fall, and there were gorgeous leaves changing colors all over the place. The main building was a white Victorian-style mansion sitting in front of a big pond. I had to stay there two nights to detox, which were pretty much a blur. However, thanks to what I wrote in my journal, the first few days were a combination of summer camp, college and prison. I felt tired, irritable, sad, hungry and frustrated (mixed with dry skin, breakouts and weight gain). Fun, huh?

Nobody wanted to be there, including a big celebrity actress I'd always thought was insanely gorgeous. We all looked like zombies and hot messes in our Juicy sweat suits, and everyone was smoking cigarettes like crazy, which was never my thing (although I'm not gonna lie, the thought of picking up smoking as a replacement habit did cross my mind—that is, until my common sense kicked in about the potential deadly and smelly side effects).

After completing my two nights in zombie land, I was sent to the Barrett House dorm with 12 other women, where I was assigned a roommate, household chores and a curfew—lights out at 11:30 pm! In addition to cell phones, here's what else was banned from the property: computers, cameras, mouthwash, hairspray, poppy seeds, weapons, porn, scales, candles, golf clubs, sexual contact, cutting hair, body piercing, eating in bedrooms, movies glorifying drugs or alcohol and caffeine after 1 pm! *Wait, what?* That's right, only decaf coffee was allowed after 1 pm, which I was sadly reminded of every single afternoon, since my household chore was to clean up the coffee machine area.

I needed to learn my housemates' stories ASAP to gauge whether I really belonged in rehab. As it turned out, their rock bottoms weren't all that different from mine—some were worse, some weren't. It was obvious I had chosen the equivalent to a white-collar prison, with mostly upscale crimes of booze and coke and hardly any homeless heroin junkies. We were all fortunate to have had the resources to be able to go to a facility like this. One woman in her late seventies claimed she'd been isolating for years inside her home, drinking wine non-stop. The same went for an older mom who told us she relapsed every year around September 11th because her son was killed in the World Trade Center attacks. Another girl still in high school said she was only there for depression issues.

I quickly found three ladies to be in my tribe. Amy was my roommate, a young party girl whose parents clearly enabled her drug use—and this was not her first rehab rodeo. She was more interested in hooking up with a guy in the house across from us. Melanie was a Parisian woman who checked in after her husband caught her hooking up with some dude in their apartment while she was in a blackout. Finally, there was Laura, a mother of three (including a one-month old baby) who needed cocaine to get through her day. She was forced into rehab by her husband, who'd finally caught on to her two-year affair with her boss. Her husband even came by every few days to collect her pumped breast-milk that was stored in our common area freezer! As a side note, all three of these women relapsed within a couple months of our stay.

My posse quickly learned that Silver Hill was not some chi-chi place for daily yoga, massages, relaxation, green juice and farm-to-table food. Instead, it was 28 long days of activities, hard work and group therapy to dissect our past behavior. Hour-long classes included topics such as the biology of addiction, defense mechanisms, codependency, denial, creative spirituality, anger management and radical acceptance. Because I knew it cost $25,000 for the inpatient stay (my insurance thankfully paid $17,000 of it), I decided I was going to do rehab right and really try, if for monetary reasons alone. This meant sitting in the front row, taking notes and participating. It really was the best money I could ever spend on myself. I went the extra mile by getting up early every day to go to the 7 am 12-step meeting in town with the "real world" people. I'd come back for meditation time, three hours of outpatient group therapy, individual counseling sessions, guest speakers and several 12-step meetings on campus at night. Sleeping all day (in the bed I was forced to make each morning) wasn't an option.

Each day went until 10 pm, but on the weekends it had more of a summer camp vibe. We made tie-dye shirts, floral arrangements, did ropes courses and played with therapy animals. There were visitor hours (a few friends did come to see me), gym time and scheduled meals in the cafeteria, which were full of carbs and sweets I definitely took advantage of. Most people do gain some weight when they first get sober because they don't have any stimulants suppressing their appetite—and food can be a comforting substitute when there's no booze to console you or drugs to numb out the pain.

That's the key point that was drilled into my head over and over again at Silver Hill, and the number one concept I remember in sobriety. Nothing is going to get better by drinking, drugging and numbing out. You're still going to have to deal with the problem when you come out of your intoxicated state—and most likely with a hangover, some depression and self-loathing too. Putting off dealing with your issues can only make them worse. I promise you: problems will go away faster if you just allow yourself to identify, grieve and *feel* them (but more on that later).

Silver Hill, as I'm sure is the case with most rehabs, strongly suggested their patients admit they had a problem with drugs or alcohol, that they were powerless over their addictions, and that they needed something greater than themselves to help overcome it, be it God, the Universe, a Higher Power or a Source Energy. I'd like to think being in rehab would be the first hint of having a problem, but hey, many people with substance abuse disorders will never even dip one pinky toe into a treatment program or 12-step meeting.

It's the question I get asked all the time: *"How do you know if you have a problem?"* I like to sum it up this way, based on what I learned in rehab, my first decade of sobriety and the more obvious signs: Do people get mad at you for how you act when you're using? Are your loved ones asking you to stop or get help? Are you in trouble with the law or at risk of being fired as a result of your drinking and drugging?

The authorities on the matter say if you don't have a problem with alcohol, then you should be able to quit booze or whatever you're addicted to for one year without any hesitancy. I think that's ridiculous, but I'm also an alcoholic. Some online articles suggest quitting for a month; however, the problem with that is it's pretty doable, and alcoholics can convince themselves or others they don't have an issue and go back to problem drinking the very next month. A year is way more severe. But for normal people, they can take it or leave it. Alcohol is like broccoli to them. They can have one or two servings and certainly don't have to think about how long it's been since their last drink—like broccoli!

"Normies," as we alcoholics call them, can deal with their problems rather than drinking them away. Anyone who's escaping everything in their life by numbing their pain, boredom and irritation with drinks and drugs likely has a problem—but there's no need to get bent out of shape about it. Just think of this quote I wrote down in rehab, which

Google can't attribute to anyone specific: "Whether I puke in the sink, or puke in my mink, alcoholism is an equal opportunity disease."

I also learned (even though it's pretty obvious) that one of the things that suffers most in addiction is our relationships, because addicts are self-centered. When I was in rehab, one of our teachers gave us a printout with 10 rules on it, just to remind us that the world didn't revolve around us. Here are four of the most compelling that are worth passing along as a reminder to everyone, really:

1. Life is not fair. Get used to it.
2. The world doesn't care about your self-esteem. The world will expect you to accomplish something before you can feel good about yourself.
3. If you mess up, it's not your parents' fault, so don't whine about your mistakes. Learn from them.
4. Television is not real life. In real life, people have to leave the coffee shop and go to their jobs.

Speaking of jobs, another question I had to answer and discuss with my group was this: "If you hired someone like you to manage your life, would you continue paying her?" In response to that, I wrote in my journal:

The woman managing my life is totally disorganized. She procrastinates and is lazy, selfish and vain. She puts her hands up when things don't go her way and hates to do work, especially when it doesn't benefit her. She needs to be fired. She's stubborn as hell!

"We cannot become what we want to be by remaining what we are."
—*Max De Pree*

Facing reality by dissecting my out-of-control behavior was one of the more unpleasant rehab assignments. I hadn't realized how much damage I'd done to my relationship with my husband. Carter was invited up for a family workshop one weekend, and he too was asked to write a letter to drugs. I kept the letter in my "rehab box," which I didn't even open for seven years. When I read his letter again, I bawled my eyes out, and still tear up about it each time to this day:

Dear Drugs,

When we first met, it looked like you had it all figured out. You were always fun, always the life of the party, up for anything, anytime, anywhere. The opportunities were endless; the world was your oyster. You were carefree and lived life like there were no consequences.

But all that fun and excitement came at great emotional cost, to your friends, family and to you. Now, the emotional bank account is drained. There's nothing left but emptiness, and when I look back at the pictures of our past, I don't see all those things I first saw when I met you. It looks more like a train wreck in slow motion.

As you drifted away, you took the love of my life with you. You and my wife were still barreling forward, leaving me behind. You were so busy living in the moment that you could not see that you were headed for the end of the line. The tracks were running out, and behind you was a path of destruction. I spent so much time picking up the pieces. I was so angry at you for leaving me behind with all the hard work while you continued on your careless and carefree journey to nowhere.

I picked up all the pieces and put them back together, but one was still missing, and you stole it from me! I want it back. I refuse to give in to your demands, so I'm taking back my life, and my wife. You cannot have either one. And I want you to keep going full speed ahead to nowhere because I don't care what you do now…

———

Ouch. Let's move on, shall we?

Another major subject covered at Silver Hill was relapse prevention. Did you know there are three stages of relapse?

Emotional relapse includes feelings such as anxiety, anger, defensiveness and isolation. This is when you're supposed to recognize these problems and change your behavior, mostly in the form of asking for help, practicing self-care, doing relaxation techniques and eating and sleeping well. *Mental relapse* is when you begin to think or fantasize about using. This stage involves glamorizing your past use, lying, hanging out with old drug buddies or going to old party haunts. To deal with this phase, you've got to "play the tape through," as they say. Remind yourself you can't just have one drink and remember all of the negative consequences that could come with a relapse. Talk to someone about the urge and distract yourself—go for a walk or take a shower. The last step is *physical relapse*, which is self-explanatory. You've driven to the liquor store or to your dealer. You've taken that shot or snorted that line. Not much you can do at this point (except maybe pray you don't overdose).

Relapse is not a part of my story since getting out of rehab. However, I did technically relapse twice before, albeit less intentionally, because I wasn't working a program then. I know what it's like to quit for a while and start back up, and it's exactly why I have to keep my experience cemented in my brain. I can't just have one drink or things will go back to how they were before. After the *World Poker Tour* spaghetti pass-out incident, I went cold turkey for nine months—except at the two-month mark, I did drink in Paris and never told a soul back home about it. We were shooting a tournament there and my co-host's friend peer pressured me into having some champagne, which then led to an all-night vodka soda affair. I spent the next three days in bed totally hungover when I could have been out exploring the city, and I even missed my excursion to the catacombs. I then felt shameful that I was lying about my sobriety. Newsflash: days still count even if you're in a land far, far away!

I managed to stay on the wagon for another seven months

after that when suddenly I found myself shooting *World Poker Tour* episodes in the Bahamas, and my same jackass friend was along for the trip again. We were out at some tiki bar and he was holding a beautiful tropical drink in his hand, begging me to join him. I remember the exact thought that went through my mind: *Well, the bosses have seen me sober for this long, and they're not here, so why not?*

It went from fruity drinks to tequila shots followed by an even worse hangover—and this time I didn't have the luxury of staying in bed. Instead, I had two or three long days of shooting and I wanted to die. I can't remember what happened when I got home from that trip, but I guess I just declared my sobriety stint was over. I don't think anyone questioned me. I know it wasn't long before cocaine came back into the picture either. Which is why when people ask me what would happen if I just had one drink, I tell them I'd immediately be seeking blow, then getting back on Adderall and Xanax too since I already fucked everything up anyways. By the way, I've never heard of one person coming back from a relapse and saying how amazing it was!

Rehab is not a part of everyone's journey to sobriety. I have friends who got sober by simply going to 12-step meetings. I also know people who got sober in jail or who decided to quit cold turkey and haven't had a single drink in over a decade. When I'm asked for advice, I always suggest rehab, not only because it worked for me, but because I believe it sets you up for success. It's easier to stay clean for 28 days when you're giving daily urine samples and being monitored 24-7. Once you have that time under your belt, the benefits start showing up: Presence. Clarity. Health.

I honestly don't know if I would have taken sobriety as seriously if I'd just done an outpatient program somewhere. Inpatient made the stakes higher for me. My bosses knew I was there. I had to take time away from work. I gave up a

vacation to go. It cost a lot of money. I had to succeed at it…
well, at least for a year!

———

National Drug Information Treatment and Referral 24/7
Hotline:(800) 662-HELP

Alcohol Abuse and Crisis Intervention:
(800) 234-0246

The drawing of my addiction at rehab

CHAPTER 4
SOBRIETY 101 (WHO THE FUCK AM I SOBER?)

"You have no idea how long a year is until you're stone sober."
—*Bill Burr*

We all know the movie *Groundhog Day*, right? It could also have been titled "Early Sobriety," because that's exactly what my first six months sober felt like. I had spent so much time in a mind-altered state that I didn't know what to do with my newfound time except sleep a lot. The days were painfully long, and I didn't like being so present with myself—probably because I didn't like myself all too much. But the revelations of my reintegration and reinvention were starting to appear.

One of the first things I noticed when I got back to New York City from rehab was everything *in* the city! The buildings, the architecture, the lights, the colors, the beauty, the people! It's like I'd been living unconsciously and never paid attention to anything except my outfits and party plans in "Courtney Land," along with my Fox News work bubble. I went from being shallow, superficial and constantly distracted to waking up and being able to focus for more than a second on my surroundings.

The same went for people and what they were saying, too. I could listen to them now! I still had to interact with my former coke buddies because I worked with most of them, but I quickly realized they weren't all that interesting and we had nothing in common except for partying. Since I could no longer offer them that, naturally they drifted away, and that was okay. I was blessed to have many friends who did support me through my sobriety journey and continue to do so to this day. However, I needed to grieve the loss of my best friend: alcohol. That part of my life—drinking almost daily for 15 years, and all the comfort and lifestyle that came with it —had died. And I was told it was okay to feel sad about it and to mourn.

But there was another passion I was losing as well: my career and my airtime. My re-entry at Fox News Channel (or lack thereof) did not go as I had hoped. Perhaps my bosses were just taking it easy on me, but I was basically put on the bench. I had been at FNC for two and a half years when I went to rehab. Up until that point I'd worked like crazy, appearing on the channel five to seven times a day, six to seven days a week. There was even an article on one of our industry blogs about how the other ladies at FNC were jealous of all my airtime. I was the news headline anchor on *Fox & Friends Weekend* (I also filled in hosting *F&F* too) and had my own segment on the daytime show *Happening Now* called "Big Click." This was right at the beginning of Facebook, Twitter, Buzzfeed and iPhones, so I'd give reports on the social media and tech news of the day. I'd get up super early, take two Adderall and search for story ideas while working out on my mini-elliptical. I'd also do reports on shows hosted by Sean Hannity, Neil Cavuto, Shepard Smith, Megyn Kelly and Geraldo Rivera. I appeared on the Fox Business Network, too. My biggest break came a few months before rehab, when I got a segment on FNC's number-one-rated show *The O'Reilly Factor* with Bill O'Reilly. It was called

"Did You See That?" and I would talk about ridiculous online videos of the week.

Since I'd disappeared for six weeks, the producer I worked with on *Happening Now* was reassigned elsewhere. There was also a big change with the executives that happened while I was away, so the new vice president of news had no clue who I was. I was replaced by another blond correspondent in O'Reilly's "No Spin Zone," which probably turned out to be a blessing considering she later ended up filing a sexual harassment lawsuit against him. Years later, O'Reilly was fired from FNC anyways, so in the long run, what did it matter that I never got to be on his show again? I'm still alive!

At the time, however, I was devastated. I could barely get on TV. Maybe once or twice a week. Losing 95 percent of my airtime *and* my love of partying was like losing my entire identity! It was beyond depressing and seriously boring, and I was never able to recover that TV time for the rest of my years at FNC. Even my twirls for Roger Ailes got me nowhere. Everyone has heard the stories by now, especially with the TV miniseries *The Loudest Voice* and the movie *Bombshell* hitting screens in 2019.

I too dealt with sexual harassment from the head of Fox News, though not to the extent some of my other colleagues did. When I would have meetings with Roger in his office (which had security monitors and a huge lock on the door), he would ask me to twirl for him. He'd always tell me I was "the hottest one at Fox," and would compliment my legs. We weren't allowed to wear pants, and if I was anchoring *Fox & Friends* on the curvy couch with the laptop screen blocking the view of my legs, Roger would call the control room and have the director tell me to shut it.

The comments and twirling made me feel uncomfortable, but at the time, I would deflect my feelings with humor, saying: "Oh, Roger just has DOMS." DOMS was a term I made up that stood for either Dirty Old Man Syndrome or Dirty Old Man Symptoms. I'm convinced all men have one or the other.

President Trump, who was just Donald Trump at the time, also told me I was the hottest one at Fox News, and even called me up on my office line with a proposition. It was 2010 and I'd interviewed him many times on red carpets, with Melania right by his side. I once told him I'd love to be a judge on Miss USA (since he owned the pageant at the time). He asked for my business card and said he'd look into it for me.

To my surprise, Trump called me a few weeks later. Though he said I couldn't be a judge since I worked at a different network, he did ask me about my career goals and complimented my work at FNC. Then, out of nowhere, he said: "You should come up to my office sometime, so we can kiss." I was shocked—seriously, who says that? "Donald," I responded, "I believe we're both married." I quickly ended the call—my office mate and colleague Rick Folbaum had witnessed the whole conversation while sitting at the desk right next to me.

Years later, this proposition made it difficult for me to report with a straight face on Trump running for president. It infuriated me that he would call all the women who shared stories of his bold advances liars. I totally believe them. At least now I can joke that I could have banged the President—but I passed. Anyway, I digress.

Sometimes in recovery, things get worse before they get better. Luckily, I wasn't facing any legal or financial problems post-rehab. I could have been resentful about getting side-lined, but I wasn't. I appreciated the fact that for my entire six weeks off, the HR department didn't make me use any of my sick days, holidays, vacation time or short-term disability.

The blessing of the downtime at Fox was that I had the opportunity to focus on my recovery. I did exactly what Silver

Hill recommended I do when I get out. I completed three months of outpatient rehab, which meant going to three-hour-long sessions three nights a week the first month, two nights a week the second month and one night a week for the third month. I went to 90 12-step meetings in 90 days and signed up for a six-month commitment to run the microphone around for people who wanted to share (felt like a natural fit for me).

I got a therapist down the street from me who I saw every Wednesday morning before work for two years. Ironically, her brownstone's windows looked out into the same back-yard courtyard as my ground-level apartment, where I previously threw loud barbeques that turned into wild dance parties until the wee hours of the morning. Let's just say this therapist was glad I got sober, as I'm sure the whole Upper West Side was too.

When my Fox contract came up around my six-month sober mark, I was offered a weekend anchor job back out in Los Angeles at the local CBS station. There was also interest in me doing entertainment reporting nationally for CBS network. I was still upset about my Fox situation, but my bosses graciously offered me another three-year contract, and I remembered another key piece of rehab advice: no major changes within the first year of sobriety! As hard as it was to do, I turned down the weekend anchor gig and decided to put faith in knowing that the same job opportunity could happen again for me one day. Sure enough, it did—I've been the weekend anchor at KTLA since 2013.

Around the same time, through divine intervention, I was hooked up with Gabrielle Bernstein, a now-famous self-help guru and multiple New York Times best-selling author. She's also Marianne Williamson's protégé and is friends with Oprah! When we met in early 2010, Gabby had four years sober and a similar usage history to mine. She ended up becoming an amazing mentor to me and I still use many of her teachings to this day.

For starters, the main thing Gabby said that resonated with me is that I'd simply lost the privilege to drink. After a 15-year party career, I'd crossed the line too many times. If you look at the situation that way, it's pretty easy to comprehend. We dissected my character flaws, resentments, fears and past relationships. Gabby also gave me this great daily prayer: *Show me where to go, show me what to do, show me what to say and to who.* She even gave me a mantra for anxious moments: *Everything is happening around me and I am taken care of.*

Speaking of anxiety, that was starting to dissipate altogether. Pre-rehab, I couldn't go anywhere for years without a bottle of Xanax on me in case I had a panic attack. I was fearful I'd get stuck underground in a broken-down subway, panicked about crazy fast cab drivers and hated flying. I needed to be drunk or take some sort of benzodiazepine before I could even take off. I'd drink the whole flight and end up doing stupid shit, like the time I made out with a married flight attendant.

I was very up and down emotionally, scatterbrained and couldn't concentrate. I realized all the chemicals mixing around in my brain were creating that anxiety for me. Now, in sobriety, I don't have any big highs or lows. Some may call that boring, but I say it's an awesome sense of calm. I'm even-keeled, content and at peace, and I certainly don't miss the drama. When I drank, I was the definition of "loose lips sink ships": *Sorry I said that, I was drunk! Sorry I made out with him or her, I was drunk! Sorry I was an embarrassing asshole at your wedding, your drinks were too strong!*

Being too drunk wasn't an excuse, but I certainly used it as one. It was never my fault—and my behavior cost me some friendships. Stopping drinking helped me gain a filter. I could now edit information before it flowed out of my mouth, both in-person and on TV too. I had a new sense of judgment and started distancing myself from gossip. Now, when someone tells me not to repeat their secrets, I keep my mouth shut. That's how you become a trustworthy person who people confide in. And it is so refreshing to wake up knowing you're not in trouble for your behavior during a blackout because you remember what happened!

Obviously, the way I was acting in active addiction was immature. Some of it wasn't my fault, according to what I learned in rehab; in early recovery, you mentally stay the same age as when you took your first drink. So, even though I was nearly 30, I was living with the maturity level of a 15-year-old. I had a lot of growing up to do.

Part of being an adult is being accountable. Accountability goes hand-in-hand with sobriety, unless you're a sociopath and your brain isn't wired with any concern for others. Getting sober taught me to show up for the people in my life and for important events. No more flaking, forgetting birthdays, calling out sick or coming up with excuses to miss plans because I was really hungover. I became thoughtful and reliable, and there's a sense of pride that comes with being responsible and following through with commitments. I also knew I had to show up for myself, own my shit and keep my side of the street clean. Above all, life became much more manageable in sobriety because there was more time to deal with the stuff I had to do—since I wasn't out there wasting all those hours on my addiction.

That's one of my favorite things about being sober: the social freedom that comes with it. It is the most freeing feeling to do whatever you want to do or not do. You can drop into a party for one to two hours and leave when you're bored and not be committed to an all-nighter you know will result in a hangover the next day. You've always got an out since you're not drinking, and you don't have to worry about how you're getting home. You save so much money by not having a bar tab, and when you split meals with friends, you often end up paying less because they know you didn't drink. It's also reassuring to know you're not going to get in trouble with the law. I have yet to be pulled over at a DUI checkpoint, even though I kind of really want to be—just so I can pass the breathalyzer with flying colors!

What I still can't seem to control are the occasional drug dreams where I get into all sorts of trouble. Drug dreams are a completely normal occurrence in sobriety. I have one probably every two months, and it's always the same storyline: I'm secretly drinking or doing cocaine and mad at myself for messing up my sober time and lying to my loved ones. Each dream feels so real and sometimes I'm soaked in sweat from the stress—as was the case when I dreamed about getting drunk, leaving my daughter somewhere and having social services take her away. Or getting caught cheating on someone while using. Or getting lost. Or trying to read the teleprompter drunk!

My friend says if you enjoy your high in your dream, which I never seem to do, it's called a "freelapse." Drug dreams are good reminders to be grateful for sobriety. I can't even tell you how relieved I am when I wake up and realize it's not true and don't have to start my time all over again!

"Sobriety is never owned. It's rented. And rent is due every day."
—Unknown

My new life was starting to seem more conducive to having a child. I'd always wanted the career and not kids, but I'd made a deal with my husband that I'd start discussing the possibility of children when I turned 30. Since I was now following up with commitments, and was turning 30 with job security, Carter and I decided I'd go off birth control to see what happened. I was basically pregnant the next day, at eight months sober. The ironic part is that for the first 20 weeks of my pregnancy, I was so nauseous that I felt hungover 24-7 and got the equivalent of drunk spins when I lay down in bed. *How is this fair?* I thought.

Being pregnant with my son was obviously a "legitimate" reason not to drink: I now had to be clean and responsible not just for myself, but for another human being baking inside my belly. Still, you'd be surprised how many people still pressure you to drink wine when you're pregnant—especially in Italy, where Carter and I did our babymoon. My answer was always: "What's the point of one glass? I'd want the bottle." Having the belly excuse did help me get through my first sober summer in NYC, because back then, I was still concerned with what others thought about me not drinking.

At restaurants, bars or parties, I would order drinks that looked like cocktails, my favorite being a cranberry ginger ale with a lime. What I eventually came to realize is that most people are not paying attention to what you're drinking anyways, and if they're pressuring you about why you're not imbibing, then they likely have an alcohol problem themselves. I know because I used to bully people with *are you pregnant, are you on antibiotics, are you on a strict diet, do you have to go to work after this?* I couldn't comprehend why people didn't drink!

That's why I just own it now. I'll straight up tell whoever asks me why I'm not drinking that I have been sober for "fill in the blank" amount of time. Those who are sober curious usually go on to ask a lot of questions about it.

I am so grateful for my son Cash. Even though it was the most miserable nine months being pregnant with him, I was rewarded with the sweetest, cutest, most sensitive and outgoing little boy who has never seen his mommy under the influence (he does see me pee my pants often, but that's just because he was a nine-pound baby and ruined my bladder forever).

I never felt very maternal, so I was surprised that I liked

being a mom—so much so that I decided to do it again, when God and Carter accidentally got me pregnant when Cash was only six months old. I was kind of relieved about my unplanned blessing because I had another excuse not to drink again for nine more months. Those combined 18 months helped me build more sober time, and the more time you get, the more confident and comfortable you feel about living substance free.

Apparently, God felt I could handle pain over a difficult child, so He dealt me another nine months of misery…but then blessed me with a daughter Carter and I named Cameron who was even cuddlier and mellower than Cash. I seriously have the most well-behaved and loving children who bring me so much joy. They are the blessings of my sobriety.

A mom friend once told me how she couldn't read a book to her son unless she had three glasses of wine first because it was such a boring task. I know many moms who are literally counting down the minutes until their kids go to bed so they can break open the vino—but I never want to be like that. I want to always be 100 percent present for Cash and Cam, and to set a good example for them.

Don't get me wrong—they're still demanding little buggers. When they're doing their loud "Mommy, Mommy, Mommy" routine, I'm so grateful I'm not hungover on the couch. I don't know how women can handle being a slave to their children while their head is throbbing and they want to puke. By the way ladies, my number one labor tip: push like you're peeing and you won't crap the table—works every time!

Hosting *Fox & Friends*

CHAPTER 5
#LOVESTORYDIVORCE

"Divorce is probably as painful as death."
—William Shatner

While I was pregnant with Cameron, Fox News asked me if I wanted to finish out the last year of my contract back in LA as the entertainment reporter at their local station. My bosses told me they wanted to make things right because they knew I'd gotten lost in the mix after going to rehab and staying sober. I was thrilled to move back to LA and to be on the air every night. I'm much happier when I stay busy and I'm not idle—the only problem with the move was that it was the beginning of the end for my marriage.

After 12 years together (compromised early on by my substance abuse), Carter and I had grown apart. We mutually decided to pull the Band-Aid off what had become a toxic relationship, and we divorced amicably in September 2014. Nothing could have prepared me for the brutal post-divorce pain I would suffer over the death of our relationship and our family unit. I sobbed non-stop for the first two years, which were the most traumatic years so far in my sober life.

Thank goodness Katy Perry talked in a magazine article about how she cried over a toilet during her divorce in order to not mess up her makeup and have her fake eyelashes fall off. This tip was incredibly useful to me as I did it too many times to count during my own divorce, both out in the field and in the KTLA studio bathroom. I specifically remember one time when my photographer and I were getting fast food somewhere in between my live shots covering a murdered high school student. My eyes were about to flood with tears, so I excused myself to the bathroom to hang my head over the toilet and let them stream down. I managed to keep my makeup intact only to return to the school where the victim's angry family member told me to fuck off. That was just one of many shitty days, and yet another time where I really wanted to drink—but I didn't.

Week after week, I choked back tears during my newscasts and bawled my eyes out on the drive home from work. For some reason, grocery stores were a major sadness trigger, and I couldn't go into them without crying. I wandered around aimlessly in Ross Dress for Less, buying things I didn't need to fill the void. Valentine's Days were spent crying so violently I thought my neighbors might call the police on me. I had a constant sensation like I was being stabbed in the chest and stomach. I don't think I've ever felt more broken or lonely. It was painful as fuck, and I just wanted to numb it all out. Instead, I took the healthier approach to cope and distract myself, primarily by attending all sorts of yoga classes: aerial, acro, on rooftops, beaches, by candlelight, and with goats—and I cried through a lot of them! I did an underwater photoshoot, floated in a sensory-deprivation tank, went trapezing, attended new moon writing workshops, went to spiritual conferences and read a bunch of self-help books. In my case, weird equaled therapeutic.

Nobody gets married with the intention of getting divorced, but we all know the divorce rate in the US is between 40 to 50 percent, depending on which study you're looking at. Not surprisingly, a lot of those divorcées are in 12-step programs. There's a joke that Alcoholics Anonymous has a higher success rate ending marriages than it does keeping its members sober. After all, alcoholics marry at the same rate as those who don't have a substance-abuse problems, yet they get divorced at four times the rate of the general population. I didn't want to be in that category, but the truth is, the dynamic in a relationship does shift when one person gets into recovery.

The week I filed and moved out was the second worst week of my life, tied with my first in rehab. I had no clue who I was outside of a relationship as I'd been in one my entire adult life—maturity stops when addiction begins, remember? I wasn't an independent self-sustaining adult when I met Carter at age 22, which led to him taking care of most of the logistics in our relationship. So, at 34 years old with five years of sobriety under my belt, I would have to learn how to do so many things: paying my bills, taking care of my new place and learning how to be alone!

"Codependency is driven by the agreement that I will work harder on your problem and your life than you do. This is not love."
—Unknown

Many years later, thanks in part to Darlene Lancer's book *Codependency for Dummies*, I came to understand how codependent I'd been. Lancer believes codependency underlies all addiction, and that you can't treat it until the addicted person is completely abstinent. Her definition of a codependent is someone with a lost self who organizes their thinking and behavior around a substance, process or other people. She gives codependent relationships two roles: top dog and underdog. The addict is the latter, with traits of self-centeredness, irresponsibility, unreliability and dependence (aka *me!*)

The top dog is overly responsible and does most of the parenting. Both feel sorry for themselves and blame one another.

According to Lancer, when the underdog addict gets sober, they typically feel guilt and shame about their past behavior. But the top dog is still harboring resentment and wants to bring up the past grievances to the now clear-headed underdog. Doing that just adds to the underdog's shame and feelings of being managed, which they can no longer numb out with mind-altering substances. In the meantime, the top dog begins losing control over parenting and enabling their partner, and may also resent the underdog or addict's new time spent going to 12-step meetings. Lancer recommends spouses get outside help to heal these deeper issues and to learn new coping and communication skills, adding that codependency is a progressive illness just like addiction.

There are plenty of great divorce blogs and online resources out there with tips about how to get better and to recover. Some of my favorite tips include forgiving yourself, leaning on supportive family or friends, getting physical, sharing at meetings, taking time off, writing it out, seeing a therapist, focusing on what you can control, and most importantly, accepting responsibility. You have to own your shit, people!

Leading up to my divorce, I'd read an article about 15 things to consider before going through with it. Two of the key points were that you have to be okay with someone else sleeping with your husband and okay with that person being around your kids. I knew both would be part of the equation, so I had to be okay with them—duh! I couldn't pick and choose. Is there a law that my ex-husband must be celibate for the rest of my life? No. Why would I be given that power? I'm baffled by how many people get upset about who their ex is dating after they've separated. It's really none of their business, unless children are in the picture. But more on that in a second.

I know many women who still expect their ex-husbands to rescue them from situations, but I refused to do that and never called Carter even once for help. I needed to be a big girl and to figure it out myself. I found myself a "handyman husband" who hung TVs, curtains, chandeliers, assembled furniture and even killed bees for me for 35 bucks an hour. When something was wrong with my car, I took it by the gas station or dealership and found someone to help me. Sure, I may have missed paying a few bills on time, but when that bright red letter came telling me my electricity was going to be shut off if I didn't pay up, you better believe I learned that lesson real fast. It's empowering to be on your own as a responsible adult!

I could have been angry and resentful like so many people who harbor hate for their ex- wives or husbands. But if there's anything I've learned in my news job, it's just how short life can be. Why not just move on? You forgive for *you*, because *you* deserve the peace—and so your body doesn't store negative energy that can turn cancerous.

It's definitely easier to divorce when no kids are involved since you can just work out the financial details and never speak to each other again. When children are in the picture, you still need to be in communication with your ex and your ex needs to spend time with the kids—so wouldn't you prefer your baby daddy or mama to be a happy person? I wasn't interested in screwing Carter financially because I wanted him to still be able to take Cash and Cam on vacations and not feed them Top Ramen. To this day, we split everything 50-50.

When you get sober and work a program, you naturally mature and want to take the high road to avoid controversy by eliminating vindictiveness, manipulation and power-tripping. No shit-talking your kids' mother or father, either.

Actress Gwyneth Paltrow and Coldplay's Chris Martin famously called their split a "conscious uncoupling." I came up with my own term. I'm having what I call a "Love Story Divorce," complete with awesome co-parenting for Cash and Cam, which now includes their stepmom.

Lauren started dating Carter about six months after we separated, and they got married in 2018. I call her my "sister wife." I truly love this woman and get asked all the time how that's even possible. For starters, she had nothing to do with our divorce. As I slowly started to get to know her, I soon saw she was a great human being and an excellent role model for my kids. They love her and she loves them. I thought it was incredibly sweet when Lauren made Cash and Cam picture albums for Christmas with all of their outings together. I got a few snarky comments about that, suggesting Lauren was trying to be their mom. She is absolutely not competing with me, and it's comforting to know if something happened to me, she would be there for them.

Then there's this: how many people get their ex-husband's girlfriend a job at their own workplace? I'm willing to bet not many, but I helped Lauren get a reporter job with me at KTLA. My coworkers wondered how I could push for her to get a meeting with my bosses (who also thought it was weird, by the way, since they both knew Carter—TV news is a small incestuous business). After I tossed to Lauren in the field from the anchor desk, an industry blog wrote an article about the "soap opera going on at KTLA." I then had to defend the situation by saying Lauren was a kick-ass reporter who fit in perfectly, and that helping her was the least I could do to thank her for being an amazing stepmom to my kids. Sometimes we even exchange the kids at work!

Carter, Lauren and I are very good about keeping the lines of communication open, and we've promised each other that we'll always discuss anything before getting upset. We share a family calendar and keep our conversations going in a group text. I don't cross the line and talk to Lauren about past issues with Carter, nor does she talk about him that way with me. We do lots of things together, whether that's holidays, birthdays, trick-or-treating or back-to-school nights. We live right down the street from each other. We exchange gifts. We're flexible on switching days with the kids and helping each other out in a pinch. Our primary focus obviously revolves around Cash and Cam. It takes a village, right?

All that being said, in the beginning years of my divorce, it was more challenging to see the two of them so happy, only because I was not in a relationship. It was also still hard to find out they were getting engaged, and I felt uneasy the night they got married. Both things happened right before anchoring four hours of news.

I was crying Katy Perry style in the bathroom until almost the last minute and called out sick the next day to have a Courtney pity party. I was also sent a test from the Universe on their wedding night when my housekeeper texted me that she'd left two bottles of wine in my fridge by accident. I went home and immediately put them in a cabinet so I wouldn't have to see them in my fridge all week. My being upset really had nothing to do with Carter and Lauren, because their nuptials were the best-case scenario for my kids and me. I took that time off work to allow myself to feel it, and then guess what? I was over everything by the next day!

Instead of lamenting what my ex and his new wife shared (the house, the ring, the vacations), I learned about the power of changing one's perspective. Rather than stewing internally and saying *that's so fucking unfair*, I learned to say (and truly feel and believe) that *this, too, can happen to me*. In short, I learned how to genuinely be happy for them, and in so doing, how to sow the seeds of happiness in my own life. I even manifested a Zen Den in my current home after seeing the Zen Den Lauren had created in the house I'd shared with Carter. At the time, I was living in a two-bedroom apartment and could have been envious, but I just kept repeating to myself: *I'll have a Zen Den too one day!* Sure enough, when the opportunity came, Lauren helped me with ideas to decorate it!

I also refuse to see my divorce like so many others do, like their marriage was a failure. Aside from getting sober, it was the best thing to happen to me. That tremendous pain I experienced forced me to work on myself, which helped me evolve into a more enlightened and spiritual person. While I hope to never go through that experience again, I'm grateful I healed through healthy grieving and got to have some *Eat, Pray, Love* moments around the world too.

Yes, my kids have a broken home—but the way I look at the situation is that now they're super lucky. Cash and Cam are living in two happy households, not one filled with fighting. They've got twice the people loving them and get to go on fun vacations with mommy, then fun vacations with daddy, plus twice the presents—they're so spoiled! And it all got even better once I found my person...

Happy Co-Parenting Halloween! Trick or Treating with
Carter, Lauren, Cash and Cam

Cash and Cam visiting Mommy on set

CHAPTER 6
COURTING COURTNEY

"Never let a fool kiss you, or a kiss fool you."
—*Joey Adams*

When I got divorced, it never even occurred to me how being sober would play a role in the dating scene. I figured it would be more of a hurdle having two young children in the mix. But I quickly learned how sober people get projected upon, and how they hold up mirrors to others—unintentionally, of course.

Not drinking wasn't a problem in my four-month rebound relationship, which happened six weeks out of the divorce gate. I was set up with a tall, dark Italian man who had an accent and was heir to his family's shipping company. On our first date, he told me he was glad I *didn't* drink since his ex-girlfriends all had booze issues, and he also believed he was allergic to alcohol because he was an American Indian in "his past life." Okay…whatever, that works for me!

Was I emotionally ready to be dating at this point? *Hell no!* But it felt good to be nurtured, given gifts, taken on trips and promised a whole bunch of shit, even if I knew deep down it would never happen. I was also the perfect, vulnerable candidate for the Italian's side job and passion as a life coach. He pushed all sorts of self-help, meditation and spiritual books on me, and decorated my apartment with healing crystals and Buddha statues.

Then out of the blue, he dumped me! When I got all Nancy Drew on him asking *why*, the Italian told me we couldn't move forward because it was clear I wasn't willing to work on myself and gave me the lamest breakup line ever: "See you in another life!" I remember immaturely texting back: "Good luck finding someone with no job or responsibilities who can just sit on a hill and meditate all day with you!" (That was before I learned how many women in LA don't have jobs aside from posting pictures on Instagram.)

I was devastated and my ego was crushed. Those blogs that say the first breakup after a divorce is the absolute worst are 100 percent correct. It took me almost a year to get over him. Thankfully, I would later come to see that the Italian was a big marker in my life, and that the seeds he'd planted set me on a path to becoming a more enlightened person.

What followed the Italian was a flurry of bad dates and me meeting men left and right—at the grocery store, at the gym, while reporting, while on planes, at church, at restaurants, in gas stations and even while stuck in traffic. Everyone and their mom wanted to hook me up with someone. At first, I attracted drunks and drug addicts—which, of course, was a deal breaker. Some dates were already wasted or high when they picked me up to go out. Others got plastered and embarrassed themselves on first dates or tried to bully me into taking a sip of their drinks.

One sports agent took me against my will on a drug run for his famous baseball player client. Another date I'd met while covering a bomb threat called me in distress to tell me his maid's child had accidentally eaten his weed and nearly died, and now social services was coming after both of them. There was also the LAPD cop who showed me videos of him performing exorcisms on mentally ill people in the back of his patrol car because he was "convinced they were possessed by the devil." My reply: "I think I'm sitting on a news story here, but I'm gonna let it slide." I later told the police chief.

Another man got really irate with me after I confronted him about the background check I'd run on him at work, which wasn't entirely surprising considering there were charges of auto theft, breaking and entering, assault and battery, evictions and liens in it. I also had a buzzed date talk non-stop about how his former girlfriend owned an orgasmic meditation studio and paired him up with more than 20 women to "rub the upper left portion of their clitorises for 15 minutes until they had a Climax 2.0!"

I needed to figure out how to look for signs of alcoholism and addiction before wasting any more of my time with shenanigans. I also could have used some better gaydar too, because apparently there are a lot of secretly gay men looking for beards in this city. But I digress.

Stalking your potential date's social media first can be a major hint. Is their Instagram feed filled with pictures of them at bars and nightclubs? Do they always have a drink in their hand? Are the photos captioned with drink emojis? Are they sending you those drink emojis during your getting-to-know-you text convos along with questions like "whiskey or tequila?" Are they telling you how hot club X, Y, Z is right now? If so, chances are that partying is a big priority to them and you'll soon be exiting stage right—so don't get too excited. As Maya Angelou said: "When people show you who they are, believe them the first time."

A common question I often get asked is *when* to tell your date that you're sober. Should you say it right away, or should you avoid drinking dates and wait to discuss the matter when you're closer with the person? My friends' unsolicited advice was to lie about why I wasn't drinking on the first few dates. "Just say you're not drinking for health reasons," one of them said, "or because you're a mom!" "Let him fall in love with you first," another suggested, "then tell him." The problem with that is I'm a really bad liar. Plus, my whole "Keep it Friel" motto is about authenticity and honesty, and all anyone has to do is check out my Instagram page to see that I'm out and proud about my sobriety! I'd rather a man remove himself from the equation immediately if he takes issue with it.

What I tried to do was schedule my first dates during the break between my weekend newscasts. This worked great because I was already glammed out, didn't have to pay a sitter or be away from my kids, was on the clock and had a reason to leave. "Sorry," I'd say, "I've got to go back to anchor the 10 pm news now!" It does help to have an out or a legit excuse not to drink, like some work event you have to go back to or an early morning meeting. My other go-to date was coffee, brunch and a power walk on the beach or a canyon hike. Kill two birds with one stone—plus it's cheap!

When you do decide to tell your date, if they give you the most disappointing look you've ever seen in your life, this is a red flag and you should run—trust me! But keep in mind how dates usually want to impress you. As such, they will straight up lie to your face and downplay how much they drink themselves. I once had a guy try so hard to convince me he was allergic to alcohol and couldn't handle more than one or two drinks. Fast forward a month later to the first time we slept together and I'm watching him down an entire large bottle of wine in five minutes tops afterwards.

I found this to be a recurring pattern with the men who made the most fuss about not liking to drink. They'll refrain at first, but once things get comfier between months one and two, the drinks start popping up more frequently. In all the above, give things time, proceed cautiously, and remember what Ben Franklin famously said: "Actions speak louder than words. Well done is better than well said."

At first, I had a hard time not taking it personally when someone wouldn't want to be with me just because I was sober. I'll never forget the handsome investment banker who ended things after a few dates: "Court," he said, "you're amazing, beautiful, funny, fun, cool, you have a career, and you've got your shit together. But I'm sorry, I just can't do the sober thing." Wait, *what?*

Surprise! Being sober is a liability for certain people. There are many people out there who believe sober people are boring, not fun and are sitting depressed and bitter in a corner somewhere. They also project onto us that we're secretly judging them or counting their drinks. Sober peeps do tend to hold a (hypothetical) mirror up to others, though not on purpose. But typically, if someone has a drinking or drug problem, they can see it while they're with us, and it makes them uncomfortable.

My best advice for not taking these projections personally, which really helped me in the dating category, came from the book *The Fifth Agreement: A Practical Guide to Self-Mastery* by Don Miguel Ruiz, the sequel to his best-selling *The Four Agreements*. The second agreement in both books is "Don't Take Anything Personally." The analogy Ruiz uses makes total sense and I'll summarize it as best as I can:

Imagine walking into a mall that has thousands of different movie theaters in it. I see the "Courtney Friel" movie playing and decide to check it out. Nobody else is in my theater except me, and I soon get bored watching my movie, because duh, I know my story. I decide to go into my mom's movie playing next door, where I see her on the screen as a totally different character. I learn she doesn't see my dad and boyfriend the same way I see them, not to mention she is the only person in her theater and doesn't even realize I'm standing in the back. As I go check out more theaters of people in my life, I realize their characters in their movies are not at all how I know them to be, nor do they even notice me in their theaters. When I get back into my movie, I realize: what does it even matter? No one sees me how I see me, and everyone is too damn focused watching their own movie to care anyways!

This is exactly why we shouldn't take things personally, because people act based on how they want the characters in their movie to play out! If they take something out on you, it's only in reaction to something going on in their story. So, if your date envisions a life where they sip cocktails at sunset every night with their future partner, then that has absolutely nothing to do with you! You could both be awesome people but simply want different things, so try not to be offended!

Having learned this information did not mean I had it all figured out, as I fell for a few more men who weren't good for me. They all looked exactly the same: six feet tall, handsome, thick brown hair and brown eyes. They were all preppy lawyer types. My friends only knew them as John One, Two, Three and Four. They were all narcissists who played games and were never going to treat me the way I deserved. But I was hooked on the sex. These guys all hated their moms, which meant their Oedipal issues made them crazy in bed. I was slapped across the face once, verbally abused, and twice had to wear long sleeves on the news to cover up my arms because there were bite marks and bruises on them from the sexcapades.

Speaking of sex, many newly sober people fear they won't enjoy sober sex or they won't be able to perform. I promise you—that's not true! In fact, I don't think I really even enjoyed sex until after I stopped drinking. It's not sloppy and the physical sensations are stronger because you're not numbed out. Plus you remember it the next morning! However, you do need a relatively present partner who knows what they're doing, because you also can't forget bad sober sex. (Drunk dudes who want to bone are obviously a no-no—ditto for having sex just because you're horny since you can't get drunk anymore, remember?)

I've found that you *must* be into the person. The times I did have sex just to have sex always made me feel bad about myself the next day. I also didn't want to turn to sex as another addiction as so many recovering alcoholics and addicts do in early sobriety. I never got to that point but I think I walked a fine line—that is until I realized I'd had enough sexual experiences in four years to last me a lifetime.

"When you stop chasing the wrong things, you give the right things a chance to catch up."
—Lolly Daskal

When I was finally willing to end my addiction to these men who were never going to be long-term, I had to dive deeper into more work on myself. I had an epiphany that I'd been subconsciously seeking out crazy dating stories to tell my coworkers because they were getting a kick out of them, and I liked being the comedian who made them laugh. I learned that I was picking men who were distant or emotionally unavailable, because I was afraid of getting rejected and hurt, of being alone or losing myself in a relationship. That, in return, gave me enough distance to be safe. I also clearly didn't think I deserved to be treated well either.

I read how to let go of expectations in the relationship chapter of the book *Letting Go: The Pathway to Surrender* by David Hawkins. Hawkins writes: "When we put pressure on other people in order to get what we want, they automatically resist, because we are trying to pressure them." Instead, if we surrender our feelings about what we want and let go of our expectations and desires, the other person then has the psychic space to become agreeable. Hawkins says we can tell if we're really surrendered when we feel okay either way about an outcome working out or not. He says doing this doesn't make us passive but active in a positive way, so we're patient and clearer to make wiser choices and decisions.

After doing a lot of work on myself, I began to see I was vibrating at a higher level of consciousness and wanted to be with someone who was open to self-help and didn't hate on the idea of spirituality. How ironic that I found myself letting people go for the same reason the Italian broke up with me! But I still wasn't telling the right story to attract the type of man I wanted and deserved. I learned this by listening to the audiobook *The Power of Your Subconscious Mind* by Joseph Murphy, which made me realize that when people had been asking me how I was doing, I'd reply with, "Well, I'm still single," or, "My life is great except for one missing part: a relationship." Murphy explained that repeating statements like that was keeping me stuck in that space.

I decided to change my approach. I came up with a new mantra to use for myself and as my answer to others: "I am enjoying my freedom until my soulmate appears!" I repeated it for only about two months, when into my life walked Jim, the most wonderful man in the world. Jim has 18 years sober, is a daily meditator and is a successful screenwriter. He's super funny, smart, laid back, and generous, and he loves my two children. Everything flows naturally with us and together we help mentor newly sober people. Remember those painful post-divorce times I spent numbing out in Ross Dress for Less? It's funny how life works, because in September 2019, Jim proposed to me at that exact same store! For real! His assistant even decorated the bedding aisle with flowers, balloons and sparkly fabric. After the proposal, my kids, parents and some friends popped out as an extra surprise. The lesson here is that next time you're feeling like you're in despair somewhere, keep in mind that something amazing could happen in the future—it did for me!

Now, does this mean that I believe the only type of relationship that works for someone sober is to be with another sober person? Not at all, although I do love that drinking isn't an issue when Jim and I travel or go out to dinner together. I know many sober people who refuse to date another sober person since they already know how an alcoholic's mind works. I say go for it if both sober partners continue to work a program and stay spiritually sound. Dating a "normie" works too, as long as they support your recovery. It just won't work with another addict because there are too many temptations involved and too much potential for peer pressure.

Here's what you should be looking for and holding out for. Memorize this quote from Sherry Argov's book *Why Men Love Bitches:* "When you meet someone who is truly great, he makes you believe you can be great, too. This is the kind of relationship you want, and it's the only kind of relationship worth having." Trust me, I thought I was going to be single forever based on what I was finding in LA, but I promise if you just keep surrendering, have faith and be positive, a healthy relationship can and will happen for you too!

OMG, did we just get engaged at ROSS?

CHAPTER 7
HEAVILY MEDITATED

"What you think, you create. What you feel, you attract. What you imagine, you become."
— *Rhonda Byrne*

Meditation...blah blah blah. My Italian rebound incessantly pushed mindfulness on me for months while we were dating and I was completely resistant to it. My typical response went like this: "You want me to hire a babysitter and then pay to sit somewhere on a floor in silence and *not* burn any calories? I am way too ADD for that—hell no!"

Thank God he did plant those meditation seeds, because once I watered them, they blossomed into beautiful lotus flowers complete with a Buddha-filled Zen garden! My meditation practice has saved my ass and is my number one tool for staying sober. I absolutely need it to stay sane and physically crave it if I've skipped a few days.

Here's how the flowers bloomed, so to speak. When things ended with the Italian, I was forced to grieve my divorce, which sent me into such despair that I was desperate for any kind of help. So when a woman at yoga invited me to try a free class with her at a new meditation studio called Unplug, I thought *fuck it, why not?* I even hired a babysitter, too.

Everything is white at Unplug Meditation. The owner, Suze Yolaf Schwartz, who happens to be a former journalist, told me the goal is to feel like you're checking into heaven—a heaven where cell phones and shoes are not allowed! In that first studio session, we all sat on cushioned chairs while the teacher, a young hip woman named Megan Monahan, sat at the front with candles and flowers surrounding her. Relaxation music was playing. It was very peaceful. *So far, so good,* I thought.

Megan began her "spiritual real talk" as she called it by holding up a jar filled with water and purple glitter. She shook it and said the glitter represented the thoughts in our head. "We have some 60 to 80 thousand thoughts swirling around in our brains every day," she said. "When you put the jar down, or meditate, it stills our minds and makes us calmer." That made sense to me. (Why didn't the Italian use the sparkle analogy—hello?)

Megan also gave us a mantra to keep repeating silently in our heads and told us to come back to it when we got distracted by our thoughts—or by what Buddhists call our "monkey minds." After all, monkeys never sit still. They're always swinging wildly from vine to vine, fretting about bananas and distracted by mating rituals. Glitter or monkeys, take your pick.

When the 40-minute class was over, I felt very relaxed and was amazed I'd been able to sit still for that long. I decided to sign up for the month-long unlimited intro special. During that first month, I was able to fit in three 30 to 40-minute classes a week and was also attempting to meditate once or twice a week at home (mostly on days I didn't have the kids). I started to list the ways my life was changing.

The first thing I noticed was that I wasn't bothered as much with events happening on the road, things like traffic or drivers cutting me off. By the time I was done saying "ass-hole," I was already over it. I remember a man yelled at me to roll down my window then screamed how I was a "stupid dumb bitch driver" for something I wasn't even involved in. I laughed back at him, asking, "Are you serious?" "Fuck you!" he shouted back. An encounter like that would have bothered me *all* day before, but instead I said, "Aww, bless you!" Then I went on my merry little Zen-ed out way.

It was the same situation when I'd end up in a long line at the grocery store or pharmacy. I didn't feel as irritated or in a rush, and just thought *whatever, I won't be here forever*. Time also seemed to be slowing down, as there were suddenly enough hours in the day to complete all my tasks. I stopped procrastinating as much and didn't wait until the last minute on tasks like getting gas, cash from the ATM or groceries. I also got way more organized and Marie Kondo-ed the shit out of my apartment.

Liking what I was seeing, I signed up for a membership at Unplug and made it a priority to go to eight classes a month for the next two years. I started noticing how present I was becoming and how I was appreciating life's moments better. I could concentrate, listen and comprehend more, and I spoke more articulately. I became better at making decisions, was less irritated by my kids, and genuinely felt happier, more adventurous, more generous and more compassionate. Healthwise, I was sleeping better, I had more energy when working out, my skin was clear and glowing, and I wasn't getting sick as much as I used to.

On the work front, I found myself not being bothered by work gossip and distanced myself from getting involved in it. I became less stressed about reporting, too. When my managers would switch my stories and send me all over the place, instead of fighting it I'd just say, "Okay," surrendering my perfectionism and acknowledging that my paycheck would still clear regardless of how my stories turned out.

I started performing better, as if I'd taken this magical chill pill that made me much more comfortable, focused and confident with my work. My bosses and coworkers noticed the change, too. As for viewer feedback or other criticism, I stopped getting all worked up about it. *That is* their *perception of me*, I would think to myself. Mine *is different and good. It's none of my business what they think of me, and I'm sorry they're in a worse place that makes them want to spew mean statements to others.*

Perhaps the biggest benefit of meditation has been that 99.9 percent of my worrying has stopped. My mind understands it can't control certain things, and by staying focused on the present moment, it keeps me from creating stories in my head. My practice came in very handy during a particular situation that rattled our KTLA newsroom for almost two years and also made national headlines.

We learned in 2016 that our parent company, Tribune Broadcasting, would be putting all its TV stations across the country up for sale. After months of rumors and speculation about who our new owner would be, Sinclair Broadcasting Group made its bid to buy KTLA. The company is very conservative, and you may recall the video montages that went viral of local news anchors at 170 Sinclair stations repeating the same "anti-media script" about the "troubling trend of irresponsible, one-sided news stories plaguing the country." Nearly our entire newsroom was freaking out at the possibility of being forced to push a right-wing agenda, not to mention the hundreds of viewers in liberal Los Angeles emailing about how they would stop watching KTLA the second Sinclair took over.

Employees at every level in every department were freaking out over rumors of longtime KTLA anchors and bosses being fired, pay cuts and format changes. Some of our talent was meeting with their union reps and talking about lining up other gigs just to be safe. Not a day went by that I didn't hear something about Sinclair. However, I chose *not* to worry about it and instead focused only on the day at hand and how grateful I was for my job. I told myself that if my contract was not renewed, I would deal with it when it happened and trust that God would place me elsewhere because I'm great at what I do.

Guess what suddenly happened in August 2018? Tribune terminated the deal to be acquired by Sinclair and sued the company for breach of contract. The takeover wasn't even happening! Imagine if I'd spent all those hours fretting over hypothetical situations, with all that worry and stress physically affecting my body? This situation reminds me of another analogy I heard at Unplug: "We are all on a train going to a destination." You can either run up and down the aisles screaming, yelling and disrupting the other passengers, or you can take a seat and look out the window. At KTLA, we were all on that train together (which ultimately broke down anyways).

Another meditation perk is the capability to remain calm in stressful situations. As I've learned, if I don't freak out, things tend to work out. For example, my son Cash split his head open in my kitchen and soaked several dish towels with blood, but I refused to think worse-case scenario. We took deep breaths together and the bleeding eventually stopped, avoiding a trip to the ER for stitches. On another occasion when my flight to Cairo was delayed and I learned I'd have to spend the night in Istanbul, Turkey by myself, instead of freaking out about the potential danger, I chose to think maybe I would find other people on the flight to go out and explore with, and began Googling things to do in that city. By virtue of having that attitude, that's exactly what happened! I found three 20-somethings to Uber into town with to see the mosques, eat kabobs, drink Turkish coffee (crazy strong, btw) and shop for jewelry and Turkish Delights (so delicious)! We had a great time and I got another stamp in my passport!

There were other key lessons I learned at Unplug as well. My teacher Megan really pushed gratitude on all the students, insisting if we weren't grateful for what we had in our lives right then, who was to say we deserved anything more? Why should the Universe give us what we wanted if we couldn't even handle what we currently had? That really resonated with me and I started the practice of writing down three things I was grateful for each day, putting them in a cute sparkly gratitude jar.

Megan also talked a lot about the importance of trusting the Universe, and how if we meditated, opportunities would present themselves without even having to do anything. For example, she said that there are ideas floating all around us and people to meet, waiting for collaboration, but we have to clear the space for them. When we make enough room inside ourselves, aka the space between our thoughts, those ideas and people will show up in our lives and come to us without our even lifting a finger. I saw this happen in my life multiple times. In fact, the title for this book came to me while I was meditating. I was able to throw a sober charity event, create sober jewelry and T-shirt lines and host my own sober show, all because random people showed up in my life and helped me do it!

My other favorite Unplug teacher, Natalie Bell, taught me how to take control of my thoughts and feelings. First of all, thoughts are fake and not real, so you must let them pass and not dwell on them or judge them. Natalie says to look at your life as if you were a mountain. Life events are the weather patterns surrounding your mountain. Just observe them passing by. There will be the occasional thunderstorm or tornado—death and other bad things—but the sun will come out again shortly. We may be shaken like an earthquake and not feel like ourselves for a while, and that's okay too. Natalie also gave me good advice during my dating escapades. If I was ever stressing out thinking about a guy, she told me to internally say, *oh, that's just my mind planning*, and bring it back to my breath in the current moment. If I felt lonely, she told me to give myself a big hug and to gently tell myself the encouraging words I wanted to hear from somebody else.

> *"Meditation is to the mind what exercise is to the body — it warms and invigorates."*
> *— John Thornton*

Okay already, you're probably thinking, *how do you meditate? Is there a correct way?* No, but you do have to be sitting or lying down in silence or with music and nothing else going on around to distract you. I've had people tell me working out, walking the beach or surfing is their meditation, but the results are just not going to be the same.

One way to meditate is to simply close your eyes and focus on your breath coming in and out of your nose and mouth. This does not keep my attention for some reason. The same goes for sitting in silence and allowing whatever comes up to come up. If I did it that way, I would just daydream or fall asleep, which does happen—and that's okay too.

I choose the mantra route. The word *mantra* is a Sanskrit word that means "mind vehicle." It's a word, phrase or sound that helps keep your mind focused by repeating it over and over. No doubt your mind will drift off to your to-do list or some other thought, but when it does, just keep going back to the mantra. I like to think of it as your brain lifting weights or going to a gym class where you can lay down for 20 to 40 minutes tops. You may not see immediate results (aside from a natural high after), but doing those mantra reps benefits the rest of your day and week. If I only have time for working out or meditating, I always choose the latter.

Some of my favorite mantras have been given to me, but I've also made up my own. I tend to repeat one four times, then switch to the next one:

"Breathe in love and kindness, exhale anger and resentment."

"Be easy on yourself, let life come to you."

"Everything is happening around me, and I am taken care of."

"Gratitude is my prayer, I can be with things as they are."

"Breathe in joy and happiness, breathe out sadness and uncertainty."

"Breathe in fruits and veggies, breathe out sugars and carbs."

More recently, I've started off my meditation sessions with a body scan. I breathe through every single part of my body and thank it for working properly and not being in pain. For example, I thank my eyelids for not having sties. I thank my wrists for not having Carpal Tunnel Syndrome or arthritis. I thank my giant knees that viewers hated on for holding me up, being strong and not needing replacements. "I breathe in health and wellness, and exhale pain and toxins!" The body scan kills about 15 to 20 minutes of time.

If you can't get to a meditation studio and want to be guided by someone, just head to YouTube. There are free meditations for almost any topic you might be dealing with or want to manifest in your life—positive energy, insomnia, anxiety, healing, wealth, happiness, intuition and—oh my—some for more powerful orgasms! If you select a visualization meditation, you'll be led through Japanese forests or along beautiful remote beaches. For me, the guides talking tend to be a distraction, but for my mom, this format is the only way she can meditate (and yes, I got her into it).

These are my three YouTube go-tos if I'm in the mood:

1. "Everything Is Always Working Out for Me" by Abraham and Esther Hicks (13 minutes)

2. "Let Go of Anxiety, Fear & Worries" on the Power-Thoughts Meditation Club channel (22 minutes)

3. "Heal While You Sleep" on the Progressive Hypnosis channel (two hours)

You can also do compassion meditation, also known as *metta*. I learned about this practice from *Good Morning America* anchor Dan Harris's book *10% Happier*, which I recommend if you want a more detailed meditation how-to guide. Dan says to pick people in your life—a benefactor (teacher, mentor), a close friend, a pet, a neutral person, a difficult person and finally "all beings"—and say to them (silently in your head, of course): *"May you be happy, may you be healthy, may you be safe, may you live with ease."*

After you've been meditating for a bit, chances are you'll have an epiphany like I did. I had a moment of enlightenment where I suddenly felt awakened, like when people claim to be born again and to accept Jesus into their hearts. I started bawling my eyes out knowing I was now seeing the world through a different lens and entering a new level of consciousness. I feel slightly psychic and am able to pick up on people's energy instantly. My intuition has also been spot-on. There's no going back to a lower state of consciousness for me (which is ironic, considering I used to brag about not being a "deep person").

I'll meditate wherever I can to fit the practice into my day, whether it be in my car, on a plane, in the news van or in a greenroom closet at work. If I miss a few days, I physically crave it and issues begin to pop up. Therefore, if I'm having a bad day, I meditate. If I have a resentment against someone, I meditate. If I can't sleep, I meditate. If I have anxiety, I meditate. It's the medicine I need in order for my life to run smoothly. In fact, everything seems to work out for me when I'm mediating a lot. I love it so much that one day I plan on getting my teaching certificate. For now, I'm teaching my kids' second and third grade classes how to do it. I'm forever grateful to Suze and the teachers at Unplug who gave me the tools and training wheels to become a kick-ass meditator on my own. I sure hope anyone reading this will give it a try—after all, what do you have to lose?

Heavily meditated

Keeping calm with Photog Rodney covering the Thomas Fire

CHAPTER 8
CAREER COPING

"Sometimes you just have to put on lip gloss and pretend to be psyched."
—Mindy Kaling

We all have to deal with stress at work, but most people don't have to talk with parents right after their children were murdered or sexually assaulted, deal with gang members flat-out telling you how they want to fuck you, or flee from homeless men spraying mace at you. They don't have to listen to emotional victim impact statements (like the mom whose ex-husband smothered their five-year-old son to death) or view pictures of men's "private parts" exploded by faulty e-cigs or cut off by cartel attacks (I'm not allowed to say the word "penis" on the air, by the way). They also don't have to view the decapitated heads of "jumpers," in news speak, who throw themselves off a bridge, the same bridge whose notorious suicide problem you just reported hours earlier on TV.

News anchors and reporters can make the job look glamorous, but I'm gonna "Keep it Friel" with you about the business. It's hard, and it's why so many people don't last in it.

It's one thing to be in the cozy air-conditioned TV studio, which only requires good teleprompter reading, alertness, energy and a strong back to keep posture in the anchor chair for five straight hours. While I'm sympathetic to the horrible stories I read from the desk, there is still a buffer that keeps me from having my empath energy zapped.

Being out in the field reporting is a whole different ball game on so many levels. Not only are you dealing with difficult topics, fast deadlines and extreme weather, but there are other elements you have to brave as well. For example, there are no toilets in the news van—and one time I had to pee in the truck's trash can because I was in the desert covering a story about human remains being found. There were helicopters flying above and no cactuses or rocks to hide behind.

I've popped too many squats to count, some caught on security cameras I'm sure, and even had to pee in someone's burnt down house because there was nowhere to go in a neighborhood decimated by the 2017 Thomas Fire (adding insult to injury). You get used to porta-potties, disgusting gas station bathrooms and knocking on doors asking random homeowners if you can go in their house. I often get carsick, and I have dry-heaved out the window on the windy roads up the mountains for snow and fire coverage.

A reporter must also have patience dealing with people, because the news van is a magnet for crazy. I recently watched my photographer John get attacked for no reason before I was about to do a live report. This angry man got off a bus, grabbed my microphone and chucked it before whipping out some mace, spraying it in John's face and biting him hard in the chest, leaving a gnarly wound. Thankfully, some LAPD officers were nearby and came to arrest the guy, who was out on probation for assault with a deadly weapon.

Another time, this cracked-out woman jumped into our live truck and said she wouldn't leave unless we gave her drugs. At least a dozen times, I've had some asshole yell "fuck her right in the pussy" behind me while I'm trying to talk live on-air. And everyone wants you to cover their personal story, which is most commonly about how they're being evicted or have had chips implanted in their brains by the FBI. My colleagues have had bleach thrown at them and knives pulled on them. Men have even masturbated (to completion) right outside their vans. Speaking of, I get dick pics and videos of men jerking off while saying my name all the time. It's super violating, and I hate checking Twitter or Instagram in the morning only to see some unsolicited junk pop up.

I'll go weeks on end where every single one of my reports is about dead people. Mass shootings are the worst to cover, and the big ones in recent years have all happened while I was on the clock. I was one of the first reporters out to the Inland Regional Center in San Bernardino where 14 innocent people were shot and killed at an office Christmas party in 2015. I had to wait with family members as they were showing up to the reunification center to see if their loved ones had been killed (and had to try to interview them too, which is never easy). When I learned the next morning that the woman I bonded with had lost her husband, I burst into tears. I had an emotional hangover. I'm still friends with her to this day, by the way, and she texts me about her PTSD every time there's a mass shooting.

We did wall-to-wall coverage after the Orlando nightclub shooting where 49 people were fatally shot in 2016. The same went for the Stoneman Douglas High School shooting in Parkland, Florida on Valentine's Day 2018, where 17 people were killed—mostly students. This was also the case in November 2018 when 12 people died in the Borderline Bar and Grill shooting in Thousand Oaks, California, which happened closer to home. Most recently there were two mass shootings within 13 hours of each other, in El Paso, Texas and Dayton, Ohio, where 31 people were killed collectively.

However, the 2017 Las Vegas massacre was the most devastatingly painful story I've covered thus far. News of the shooting at the Route 91 Harvest Music Festival broke during my newscast. So many false reports of multiple shooters at different casinos up and down the Vegas strip were floating around online. It was terrifying, and I had so much anxiety trying to remain calm on-air. We learned overnight that 58 people had been killed, and 35 of them were from Southern California. For the next two weeks, I was immersed in the national tragedy, both in LA (spending 12-hour days chasing down anyone who knew the victims) and on-site in Las Vegas. I broke down crying in my cubicle as I was putting together a victims' profile piece. How do you write about 35 people's lives in a three-minute report? A sentence on each person wasn't fair to them.

I also lost it on-air another night when we aired a montage of the victims' pictures with music. When the camera cut back to me, I was sobbing and could barely get out my next sentences, then struggled to finish the rest of my show. The moment I left the set, I cried in the bathroom, bawled my eyes out the entire car ride home, and sobbed loudly and uncontrollably on my bedroom floor for hours. I knew the victims' families had it worse, but I couldn't just turn off the news coverage like a regular viewer. I was in it, and I needed out. I wanted to jump out of my skin and escape the emotional overwhelm. I debated calling the work crisis hotline but knew whoever answered wouldn't be able to relate.

I believe this is one of the reasons why so many people drink in the news biz—to numb out these depressing issues. Since drowning my sorrows wasn't an option for me, I had to remind myself that drinking or drugging wouldn't make the situation any better, and that this too would pass. I decided to call out sick the next day because I didn't think I could mentally or physically handle reporting on the story again. Once I ate some carbs, took a shower, and got 12 hours of sleep, I felt better. It was okay to be sad, and by dealing with my feelings and grieving, they ultimately passed faster—plus I stayed sober.

I dread the next mass shooting. It's not a question of *if* it will happen, but when. I wish we as news organizations could all band together and refuse to report shooters' names. I can't remember one person who died in the Las Vegas massacre, but I know exactly who murdered them all. I've stopped saying their names. I feel we do a disservice by giving shooters so much airtime and it incentivizes future lunatics to get fame before dying themselves or being carted off to life in prison. When sports networks banded together to stop airing streakers running across the field, the problem pretty much stopped. Just saying…

As you can clearly see, the likelihood of me having some sort of bad day when reporting is high. I also sympathize with first responders, police officers, lawyers, therapists, crisis counselors and medical examiners who witness gruesome scenarios and deal with all the terrible details. Luckily, I'm able to recognize the times I previously would have been driven to drink after a stressful day. In those cases, I go home and meditate or drive myself to the beach for a powerwalk. Stress comes in all forms and is sometimes extreme beyond all measure, but I've learned to cope with it, even though I still suffer from the occasional "newsmare"—my version of a nightmare.

"Your work is going to fill a large part of your life, and the only way to be truly satisfied is to do what you believe is great work. And the only way to do great work is to love what you do."
—Steve Jobs

Part of coping with job stress meant becoming preemptive about my situation. For starters, I had to completely dissect every aspect of my job and be grateful for it. When I was at

Fox News Channel, I primarily covered entertainment and interviewed hundreds of celebrities, from Angelina Jolie and Ryan Gosling to Taylor Swift and Katy Perry. My favorite celebs to interview were Dolly Parton and Bryan Cranston— but they weren't all good.

The worst interviews were Britney Spears, who could barely get out any words, and Hank Williams Jr. The latter was wasted during a live interview and blew cigar smoke into my face while I was eight-and-a-half months pregnant. Then he hawked a loogie that landed on my purse and walked away mid-sentence!

I had a hard time transitioning from red carpet life back into gritty local news, and frankly I hated it. But when I got divorced, I knew I needed to keep my job to support my children, so I had to make myself love it in order to not be miserable. I needed a big attitude shift because I had a case of the "wants." I call this first trick "the mindfuck," and I advise you to do it as well if you're struggling with where you're at in your career or in the game of life.

I realized I was grateful my news director gave me the chance to get back into hard news because I could have been pigeonholed into the entertainment beat. I was grateful for a set schedule where I didn't have to travel at the drop of a hat, nor did I have to be on-call, which meant I could always be home for my children. I was grateful for the eight to 10 hours of exposure I was getting anchoring on the weekend, which has led to me landing TV and movie roles as a reporter and anchor (most notably on *Veep*, *Goliath*, *Agents of Shield*, *American Horror Story*, *SWAT*, *Triple XXX: Xander Cage* and *Kong Vs. Godzilla*).

I had always felt kind of stupid as an entertainment reporter and now congressmen and women and other people of authority were following me on Twitter and taking me seriously. I was getting to learn all aspects of how the city of LA is run, along with information about all sorts of topics that keep me interesting as a dinner guest! I thought about how there are thousands of people who would kill for my job and that I better damn well appreciate it! I was also grateful for the fans who followed my career and enjoyed my storytelling.

I discovered another life-changing tool that came my way through life coach Tony Robbins. Robbins asserts that the quality of your life comes down to the quality of the questions you ask yourself. For example, if you ask a question in a negative way, such as "why do bad things always happen to me" or "why can't I lose weight or make more money," you get stuck in that negative space and nothing changes. But if you ask questions that challenge your brain in a positive way, like "how can I lose weight and enjoy the process at the same time," you give it more bandwidth and energy to look for the answers to change. In fact, you even pave the way for change to manifest in your life.

I created my own mantra of questions which I now say out loud to my photographers when I get in the news van: "Who are we gonna meet today? What are we gonna learn? Who can we help? How much fun will we have? How empowered will we feel? And how low-key and low-stress of a day will we have?"

Usually one if not more of those questions is answered as we shift our perspective from negative to positive! The days I've forgotten to say the mantra have ended up being chaotic, but when I do say it, things always run smoothly. It's completely changed my outlook on reporting—and the photogs love working with me because they know we are "mantra-protected." (I even met Tony Robbins once during a news story and told him how this changed my life —gratifying!)

I rely on God to give me strength throughout the day. My parents dragged me to church every Sunday growing up, so I can thank them for the faith and moral values I have today. I know many alcoholics, and people in general, have issues with God and Jesus, but they are definitely my main homies! I listen to K-Love radio on my way to work, a commercial-free station that plays contemporary Christian music and sends uplifting messages. When I find myself in horrible situations, like the time I had to listen to 20 parents talk about how their kids were all murdered, I silently ask God to help me get through it. The same goes for when I'm in court being forced to listen to awful details of how little kids were killed.

I also tell myself that these stories need to be told and that I have been chosen to tell them. We are not sensationalizing death and destruction for ratings (at least, I don't exaggerate with my reports—I tell it like it is, and that's why viewers tell me they like and believe me). In fact, most of the disgusting and horrific details I hear about in cases are too gruesome to report on TV. We're letting future asshole parents know that if you torture your child, throw them out in the dumpster, or fry them in the microwave, there will be consequences—and Child Protective Services better be doing their job, too. In the case of little Gabriel Fernandez, the eight-year-old boy who was beaten, shot, burned, starved, forced to eat kitty litter and locked in a box, both his mom and her boyfriend were convicted of first-degree murder. Four social services workers are set to stand trial for allegedly ignoring warning signs of Gabriel's abuse as well.

Finally, I take comfort in knowing I have the ability to help people with my current job way more than when I covered entertainment news. As a result of my stories, I've gotten a cochlear ear implant for a little boy, raised $82,000 for a little girl who needed cerebral palsy surgery, found a baseball field for a blind baseball team to practice on, helped catch several killers, found missing dogs and spread important information about changes happening in Southern California. I also hope that when I do report on horrible freak accidents and incidents, it reminds people to cherish their life and loved ones, because if there's anything I've learned in this job, it's that life is short. I try to honor the people who have died in my stories to the best of my ability, too.

Since we're on the subject of careering sober, I want to discuss the topic of employers knowing about their employees' sobriety, or lack thereof. I have been asked time and time again why I publicly put it out there that I'm sober. Aren't I afraid of my bosses or potential future employers knowing? Why am I reminding people of how I used to be if I'm not like that anymore? First of all, I don't recommend publicizing your recovery until you have some sober time under your belt and are sure you want to continue living sober. Posting pictures with hashtags like #SOBERAF or doing interviews about it can be a disservice. Remember when actor David Arquette went on Oprah fresh out of rehab to preach his new sober lifestyle only to relapse shortly thereafter? Ditto for news anchor Elizabeth Vargas, who did a major primetime special with her network right before she, too, relapsed.

Once it's out there, there's no going back—but this also helps me stay accountable. You control the message about yourself, so own it! People will rally behind you, just like my KTLA coworkers did for me. I don't preach, judge or try to convert anyone, and in return, they don't shame me at the office Christmas party for not imbibing. Instead, they congratulate or celebrate with me on my sober birthdays.

I choose to believe that companies want to have employees who are not drinking and drugging and who are the best version of themselves. If they don't, that's why I'm writing this book—to help erase the stigma. Because when people stop drinking, they become who they were always meant to be. Sober people are assets! They aren't wasting all their extra hours getting fucked up, so there's more time for self-improvement and being productive, helpful people in society. Are bosses afraid they will relapse? Hello, how many current alcoholics and addicts do companies presently have working for them hungover or doing drugs on the job, living in an erratic and not-present state of mind? They would probably know if they drug-tested more, but many choose to turn a blind eye, especially in TV. As long as the talent or producer shows up for the newscast and gets good ratings, it's all good…at least, until somebody overdoses. I still can't believe I've never taken a single drug test at any of the dozen television stations I've worked at!

My news director Jason Ball is incredibly supportive of my sobriety. He rappelled down a 26-story building with me for the addiction non-profit organization Shatterproof, had our news chopper film us from up above, and let me air a story on it too. He greenlit my video podcast "Keepin' It Friel: Conversations on Recovery," and also got KTLA to donate to my sober charity event. I am so grateful for this, and I hope more bosses will follow in his footsteps.

If I *were* to ever be fired or not hired somewhere because I'm sober, or for writing this book, then it wouldn't be a place I would want to work anyways. I just have to keep the faith that that won't ever be a news headline in my story.

With my News Director Jason Ball after we rappelled down a 26-story building

My favorite celebrity of all time is Dolly Parton

Telling Tony Robbins my work mantra

Grateful for my co-anchors: Rick Chambers, Kaj Goldberg, Steve Hartman

CHAPTER 9
#FRIELTHEPAIN

"The greatest evil is physical pain."
—*Saint Augustine*

If one more person asks me if I've taken Advil for my headache, I'm going to punch them in the face. This dumb question, along with "have you had it checked out," comes *after* I explain that I've had a chronic migraine every waking moment since August 2017. If you felt like someone was sticking a knife in the top of your head and twisting your brain 24-7 for over two years, wouldn't you "get it checked out" or do everything you could to try and solve the issue?

Then there are the annoying know-it-alls who hound you to try their "healer" or think they have the solution. They may mean well, but I've literally tried dozens of these referred healers, with the only results being a drained bank account (I've spent tens of thousands of dollars on the problem). Attempting to manage my constant headache and find the cause of it has become my side job and the bane of my existence. And yet I've stayed sober through it.

Chronic pain, in any form, is depressing and debilitating. One in six people are living with it, and migraine headaches are considered to be in the top 20 disabilities, according to the World Health Organization. I wish I could say that being sober cures chronic pain, but sadly, it does not. I've found myself many times driving on the road wishing a Mack Truck would just slam into me, since I can't be an asshole and kill myself when I have two children and so many people in my life who care deeply about me.

I've missed weeks of work and had some close calls on-air too, like the time my headache was so severe it was mimicking stroke symptoms. My co-anchor thought I was having a heart attack because I was gasping for air. I didn't have enough breath to get through the stories and during the first commercial break I just started bawling my eyes out, overwhelmed with fear. The assignment desk called the paramedics to come check me out, but I knew it was just my imaginary tumor I've named "Fred" raging at a 10 on the pain scale.

One might think I'd be trying to score Vicodin, Percocet or other hardcore muscle relaxers for the pain, and I'd even have a legit reason. But amazingly, I don't want them—not to mention the last thing I need is to be sleeping on a couch all day, slurring on the news or being totally out of it with my kids.

It's a far cry from my old self, but I like being in control now and certainly don't want to jeopardize my sobriety or become dependent on a questionable chemical. The crazy thing about this is that when I was in rehab, one of our assignments was to pick the top reason we might relapse from a list of a dozen choices, such as the death of a family member, losing a job, moving, and so on. I picked pain because of my past experience with chronic headaches, but I dealt with it much differently then. Let's rewind.

In my early twenties, I had the same twisting knife sensation every single day for three years straight. Not getting any relief from the traditional medical establishment, I turned to my Latina classmate and friend's suggestion of trying out one of her Soma pills, a powerful muscle relaxer. She was from Mexico and got her supply at pharmacies in Tijuana. The pills were white and round. After chewing them so they'd enter my bloodstream faster, I instantly turned into Jell-O and felt my pain dissipate. I had found my lifesaver, even if it meant getting loopy and passing out for a day! What did I really have to do anyway, except go to class? There were a few problems with this though. I quickly built up a tolerance, I was becoming addicted and I lived in San Diego, not Tijuana.

In no time at all, I learned the route into Mexico and which *farmacias* to get my Somas at. In the early 2000s, you could just drive or walk across the border without a passport, and Tijuana wasn't as dangerous as it is now. My usual routine included grabbing a friend to drive down with me, buying 100-pill bags, sticking them into each side of my bra, and stopping at a large dance club with flashing lights and insanely loud music for quesadillas and margaritas. I also became friends with a pharmacist named Miguel, who provided us lots of free cocaine that we'd all snort together in the back room. I'd buy a fake Prada or Coach purse in a sketchy alleyway, pick up a few bottles of duty-free alcohol, then walk or drive back through the border checkpoint. I'd have all the confidence in the world to answer the US custom agent's question: "Are you an American Citizen?" *Yessssss, I am Mister Occifer!*

I now look back on those years and see how insane people can become to stop their pain, whatever it is. I thank God I never got hooked on powerful opioids, which often leads people to heroin use after their legal supply runs out. According to the DEA, 80 percent of new heroin abusers became addicted to opioids by misusing prescription medications. I've learned more extensively about the problem through reporting on stories with the Los Angeles DEA and even going on a ride-along to a big opioid bust—ironically enough, they've asked me to speak at their drug awareness summits, too!

The opioid epidemic is out of control and the numbers are staggering. As of January 2019, more than 130 people die each day from opioid overdoses, and that amount has risen every year since 2002. A recent report from the US Department of Health and Human Services shows opioid abuse among people 50 years and older is increasing too, nearly doubling over the last decade. According to data from 2016, some 11 million Americans abuse prescription drugs every year.

Just because you're sober doesn't mean you can never have another painkiller or mind-altering sub-stance again. It just needs to be for a legit reason like having surgery, and it needs to be administered or prescribed by a doctor. After I pushed out my nine-pound baby boy, it felt like I'd been slammed in my hoo-ha with a sledgehammer, and I did have a few Percocets at the hospital for the pain. When I was in labor with my daughter, my OB-GYN gave me something for the contractions that made me feel really loopy. I've also been in the emergency room twice with a pain-level-10 migraine and was treated with a morphine-like drug through an IV that made me very woozy. But those were my only "free-lapses" in an entire decade.

I make it a point to let all my doctors know up front that I'm in recovery and that I take my sobriety very seriously. This keeps them thinking outside the painkiller box, because we all know it's an easy go-to. According to the CDC, over 61 million patients in the US had at least one prescription for opioids filled or refilled in 2016! Some medical professionals, like my two neurologists, won't even deal with potential drug seekers. They filter them out right off the bat by making new clients sign a form explaining that they won't be prescribed narcotics—and that they shouldn't even ask!

If you are prescribed an opioid in sobriety, obviously there are some dos and don'ts if you want to avoid a relapse. The most obvious is to follow the directions on the label—duh! Never take more than the prescribed amount. If you can't trust yourself, give the bottle to a friend, neighbor or family member and let them hand you the medicine as directed. Don't crush up pills, especially if they're extended release.

When the pain stops hurting, stop taking the medicine! If you're tempted to order extra drugs online or go to different medical professionals for the same prescription, know that that's called doctor shopping, and your insurance will likely not pay for the same drug twice anyway. It should go without saying that taking drugs from people's medicine cabinets is a big no-no, but according to the DEA, it's how the majority of abused prescription drugs are obtained (which is why the agency has started nationwide prescription drug takeback events for better disposal options).

This time around with my headache situation, I *was* prescribed mild muscle relaxers and took them as directed, but they did nothing for my pain and instead made me prison-camp tired. I know my Soma abuse in my early 20s did nothing to solve my headaches back then either, and possibly even prolonged the issue. According to Dr. Mel Pohl at the Las Vegas Recovery Center, opioids tend to make pain worse because they backfire. It might seem like they're working pretty well, but they're actually causing inflammation in the part of your brain that elevates pain levels! This is a serious drawback—not to mention the chance of getting addicted to them. Dr. Pohl says people taking opioids for 10 days have a 21 percent chance of still being on them in a year. Take them for 30 days, and you're 22 percent more likely to still be on the drug in three years.

This is why Dr. Pohl's recovery center is one of the few in

the country that focuses on the physical, emotional and spiritual problems of those living with chronic pain. He reassures his clients that pain is real but believes that emotions drive the experience and advises alternative methods to deal with it over meds (many of which I have tried). These methods include chiropractics, physical therapy, massage, Reiki, hypnotherapy, individual therapy and exercise. Dr. Pohl says research shows that yoga gives the same benefits as drugs. I wish that were the case for me, as I do yoga, workout with my trainer regularly and went for months to a chiropractor and acupuncturist, the latter of whom also tortured me by cupping my back and piercing my ears with semi-permanent needles. No relief, unfortunately.

One of the other reasons I've had to stick with a more holistic approach to battle my headaches (aside from being sober) is that Western medicine hasn't been helping, and sometimes even makes things worse because my body is so damn sensitive. Every time I try the latest migraine medicine, hormone pill, or other anti-inflammatory or preventative prescription, it intensifies my pain even more. I had to stop getting IV infusions, nerve blockers, steroid facet injections and rounds of Botox in the crown of my head and neck because I was so sick of needles. My veins are super small, and I end up being pricked three times before the nurse can get to my blood. It's pure torture!

I've tried Chinese herbs, natural vitamins, essential oils and CBD. Quitting coffee, sugar and carbs didn't help, neither did the arsenal of headache gadgets I've bought—including ice helmets, ear pressure squeezers, neck pumpers, plug-in massagers, special NeuroLens glasses and the sexy night-guard my dentist hooked me up with to stop grinding my teeth. My latest device is an Oxygen tank on wheels—it's like I'm 80! I've also tried "spiritual colonics." That's right: a healer named Li "talks to my angels" while literally sucking the shit out of me with her colonic gizmo. It gives me clarity, a flat tummy (for, like, a day) and seems to keep my headaches at bay—at least, it alleviates some of the pain. Li tells me she can still see remnants of my addiction inside my body then proceeds to do her work, cutting energetic cords and re-balancing my chakras while she covers me with healing crystals and singing bowls.

"I'm so awesome, even my migraines can't get enough of me!"
—@TheDailyMigraine

In the summer of 2019, my head pain got so bad that I ended up taking two months off work. I needed to see if my years of non-stop death reporting were somehow manifesting pain in the top of my head. During that period, I was in bed most days with my ice helmet on and trying different tactics with a team of doctors. I dove into the self-help world too. I completed the 40-day Miracle Project, created by author Melody Beattie, where you write down 10 things you're grateful for each day for 40 days and are supposed to receive a miracle (maybe next time it'll work?).

I got a membership on the Curable app, which has you do writing exercises to your pain and about past traumas and provides podcast interviews with people who cured them-selves with the mind-body approach. It's surprisingly comforting. I've watched dozens of Abraham Hicks videos on YouTube, creating my "focus wheel" and getting "in the vortex" with some new mantras for my meditation sessions—phrases like "breathe in health and wellness, breathe out pain and toxins" and "help is on the way; this too shall pass."

After getting no relief and being insanely bored, I decided it was better to be distracted by work—not to mention I needed my full paycheck. Apologies if I'm boring you with my myriad of trials, but as you can see, it's been a fucking exhausting journey and a challenge to learn how to cultivate a relationship with my pain. As I write this book, after trying everything under the sun for over two years, all I can do is spiritually surrender. I get down on my knees daily and pray to God (usually in tears) asking that He will one day help alleviate my pain. I thank him for it as well then turn it over, since ultimately, it's out of my control.

I have to force myself to remember what my mentor Gabby Bernstein said at one of her LA speeches: every time I think I've already surrendered hundreds of times and all this positive thinking and praying isn't helping, I must surrender some more and take my hands off the wheel. *My* plan is in the way of *God's* plan. If He wants me to live in perfect health, then it will be. I must trust that whatever is in the highest good is in the plan for me and be receptive to that. Even though it's painful to be alive right now, I have to lean into the joy and dwell in the greatness of what is right now. Gabby also recommends I call on the Archangel Raphael for help. He's the angel of healing, and I believe Raphael has gotten me through some difficult days.

The Bible backs this up too. I was at a memorable sermon given by Pastor Rick Warren at Saddleback Church back in September 2018. Warren said the greatest enemy in life is fear (namely that my headaches will never go away), and that there are no comebacks without setbacks. Each setback is a setup for a comeback, so they shouldn't scare you—setbacks are just God showing up in your life. Setbacks like my pain are not intended to punish me, but to prepare me for my next stage of responsibility, and to build character and faith.

Warren went on to explain how there were even fears and setbacks with the birth of Jesus. Mary faced the fear of inadequacy (as it wasn't a planned pregnancy, obvi). Joseph faced the fear of shame (um, whose kid is this really, Mary?). The shepherds feared unexpected change, King Herod feared losing control and Zechariah feared being disappointed. Pastor Warren says we can replace our fears with faith by praying with two Bible verses. One is Luke 1:38, which reads:

"I am the Lord's servant, and I am willing to accept whatever God wants for my life." The other is Psalm 56:3-4, which reads: "When I am afraid, I put my trust in God. And when I trust in God, I am not afraid!" Warren added that one way to do this is by listening to worship music, which wasn't totally my thing before. But thanks to K-Love radio, I discovered some songs kept me from plowing my car into a tree. My personal favorites if *you're* going through a setback are Danny Gokey's "Haven't Seen It Yet," Hillary Scott's "Thy Will," and "Even If" by MercyMe.

My mom always worries about my pain and says she feels so bad for me because of it. I have to remind her what I tell myself: *I am so blessed. I have everything I need. I don't have a tumor, or cancer. I have my arms and legs, my vision and hearing. I haven't died from this and things could be so much worse!* She says I'm always too positive—but seriously, what is living in the negative going to do for me except keep me in pain?

It's like when I finally met someone in the flesh who had the same non-stop headaches as me. The woman had moved to LA from NYC to see if a change in environment would help cure her six-year constant headache. As we swapped war stories, she kept referring to herself as "getting sick." When I questioned her about why she used that phrase, she explained that this was something disabling that happened to her and that it was ruining her life.

While I totally got where she was coming from and considered using the phrase "I got sick in August of 2017" myself, I ultimately decided I would never label myself that way. I feel it robs people who can't walk, or those who can't get out of bed, breathe or eat on their own. After all, I cover stories all the time about people who are legitimately sick and dying.

I am fortunately still alive and still sober, and I refuse to be a victim. Some days are better than others, and I just have to take things moment by moment for now. Basically, I have to keep calling up my inner *Unbreakable Kimmy Schmidt, dammit!* One day I won't have this pain. In the meantime, however, I will happily accept your prayers to help speed along the process!

Trying out a hyperbaric chamber

One of the many reasons to keep living: the Friel family

CHAPTER 10
#FRIELTHEFUN

"You'd be surprised how much fun you can have sober. When you get the hang of it."
—James Pinckney Miller

'm dancing with a girlfriend at a Santa Monica nightclub when this guy comes up to me and asks: "How much cocaine are you on?" Though I'm seven years sober at this point, I realize this is probably his tactic to look for blow. I reply: "OMG, I'm high on life but thank you, that is the best compliment!" I fooled him since I was smiling and radiating such happy energy, because guess what? It *is* possible to have fun being sober!

However, attempting to dance sober for the first time was a different story. That happened during week three of rehab when I was allowed one overnight trip to be in my sister's wedding in Pennsylvania—why do weddings and rehab always go together like in the movies? I felt like a stiff robot with no moves, energy or personality. I was a hollow shell. It wasn't fun, and I ended up leaving the reception early to go to bed. But hey, at least I didn't cause a scene like at all the previous weddings I'd attended as a bridesmaid or guest—

like breaking things, undressing, insulting people, passing out or barfing, you know?

I was way too new in the game for that wedding dance session, but like most difficult situations in life, you've got to "give time time" as they say in 12-step programs. Another way is to think of the TIME acronym, which stands for "Things I Must Earn." You can't expect to be comfortable overnight. I learned that the hard way by going to Miami for a girls' weekend when I had only five months clean. The ladies were wasted by 9 am, and after I watched them drink at bars and clubs all day until 2 am, I just started crying.

My sober girlfriend, who was supposed to be my companion on the trip but ended up ditching me for a guy she'd sat next to on the plane ride down, finally showed up at the club and told me this would be the hardest sober night I would have. She was right. I just learned in that moment that I wouldn't be able to put myself in certain situations—not because I'm afraid I'll drink, but because there's a time limit for how long I want to hang out with drunk people. A 10-hour day on a yacht with an open bar? I'll pass, but thanks for the invite!

I guarantee the number one reason holding most people back from giving sobriety a try is that they believe they will never have fun again. I've heard it countless times and have also been interrogated by people who think I'm lying about living a sober life that includes fun. My friend's husband refused to get sober because he thought he'd never have fun again—now I wonder how much fun he's having buried underground in a coffin after his drug overdose.

In the beginning, I too thought life would be majorly boring without substances. After all, I drank before or during almost every single location and activity—at the mall, the movies, or plays; on boats; at mini-golf, bowling, softball and volleyball games; at charity events; during breakfast, lunch and dinner. I spent tons of money on different things I had no recollection of afterwards.

Here's what the newly sober or sober curious with this mindset are not thinking about at the time: how their *current* drinking and using hasn't really been all that fun and isn't working for them anymore. Waking up hungover every day and looking in the mirror crying about how you want to die sounds like a blast, right? It's the definition of insanity— doing the same thing over and over again, expecting a different result. In my rehab journal, I wrote this about my so-called "fun" drinking and drugging:

I was the lush, hot mess, class drunk, who would puke, pass out, black out or be slurring and embarrassing myself, compromising my values, with a head-throbbing hangover. I was argumentative, gossipy, loud and obnoxious. I drove drunk, swam drunk, fell down stairs and cut up my legs, waking up with scraped knees and bruises all the time. I broke the law and lied to those I loved, mostly by stealing and hiding pills.

Damn, who wouldn't want *me* as their party guest? I was so much fun—*not*! I could have died, gotten arrested for buying blow or driving under the influence, gotten raped, or been filmed doing something incredibly asinine on camera and fired from my job—all in the name of fun!

There's a saying on this subject in Alcoholics Anonymous that I refused to believe for my first few sober years: "Your worst day sober is better than your best day drinking." *Oh, Hell no!* I thought. *I had tons of fun drinking, and some of the best days of my life were spent on boats!* But around five years into my sobriety, I started to understand what this meant. My mindset and mental health on any bad day sober is in a way better place compared to the hot mess I was on any fun day of partying. In reality, my "best day drinking" (and snorting coke) on a yacht in Florida comprised of me peeing in the *Scarface* pool on private property and stealing some chick's Chanel sunglasses. Classy. Funny side-note about yachts: I recently had a relapse dream where I was stuck on one in cramped quarters with tons of booze and drunk people. It was a horrible nightmare, and if that situation were to happen now, it *would* be in my "worst day sober" category—LOL!

Another statement I heard in the rooms of AA that came true for me was, "your definition of fun just changes when you get sober." This is so true, I promise! The appeal of being out at a club all night turns into the joy of a morning power walk in nature, quality dining with friends or reading a book in a hammock on the beach. I now love relaxing and being pampered. I used to hate wasting time on massages, facials or pedicures, or on going to the spa. I thought it was stupid when I would do it at bachelorette parties and never liked people touching me—I would've rather been getting my drink on!

Now, hitting up a spa (especially a geothermal one) or a sauna and steam room is like going to a nightclub! I will happily pay $25 to use the Korean spa facilities, then have a lady in her bra and underwear roughly rub me from head to toe with salt scrubs. I also love the more obvious perks of sobriety: not waking up hungover, with acid reflux, feeling depressed, nauseous, anxious, dehydrated, or constipated, and being able to get right to working out and meditating!

The time that was once wasted on substance abuse is now spent engaging in new hobbies like painting or Spanish class, as well as my favorite endeavor: traveling. I get a natural high discovering the beauty, culture and history of the world—and I do it low-budget, too, flying in the last row of the plane if need be.

During my early sobriety days, I remember thinking: *what if I want to celebrate my 50th wedding anniversary in Italy with a glass of champagne?* First of all, that's called "future tripping." It's one day at a time, remember? Second, I can report back that on all of my big trips overseas since getting clean—which include Iceland, Egypt, Japan, South Korea, Colombia,

Hungary, Portugal, Italy, Turkey, Greece, Spain, London, Costa Rica, Panama, Puerto Rico, and multiple Mexico trips— I did not want even one drink.

I was completely content exploring, people-watching and having adventures at mud-volcanoes, cenotes and catacombs. I was ziplining in the rainforest, canoeing the Bio Bay, holding monkeys, beekeeping, honey-tasting and camel-riding—the weirder the activity, the better. #FrielTheWorld. On the other hand, my drunken vacations—including three memorable times in Rio De Janeiro—were spent at bars and clubs with dangerous after-hours trips into the *favelas*, Brazilian ghettos, for blow, followed by hangovers spent in bed the next day.

There's also fun to be had with children, should you choose to have them (hint, hint: living sober is a much more conducive lifestyle for raising them.) You get to relive your childhood, and watching kids experience and excel at activities and make memories is a joy I never knew existed. Trust me, I was *not* a kid person and never wanted any before I got sober. I had no idea how awesome and loving children can be. Having my son and daughter has been the biggest blessing of my sobriety (even if they cause me to constantly pee myself). You become a less selfish and more considerate person. Yes, they're a lot of work too, but being sober keeps me calm and patient with them—plus they know I'm a 100 percent present Mom, which is rewarding.

It does take a minute to discover who you are as a sober person. Ironically for me, I've come back to being the outgoing person while sober that I initially drank alcohol to become. Make sense? I promise being sober does *not* mean that you're banned to a social wasteland either. Sober people are not all bitter, boring, miserable bumps on a log who don't want you to drink in front of them! My boss asked me to discuss this topic in my book. Please, go ahead and order whatever drinks your heart desires. I don't care, and I'm not judging you or sitting there salivating over your martini or glass of wine. If anything, I'm so relieved I'm not drinking.

I don't have any sober friends who can't go to a dinner or a bar with people drinking next to them. In the first few months, you might want to stay away from it, but once time goes by, I believe most healthy sober people have zero problem with this. If the drinkers turn into slurring drunk assholes or blatantly keep hitting on us, then we will just leave—trust us! Now, I might feel differently if someone whipped out blow and started doing lines in front of me, but amazingly, in 10 years of sobriety that's never happened, and I haven't even physically seen cocaine at all! Pretty cool, huh?

I do have some tips for newbies wanting to reintegrate back into the social scene sober: Go late to the party or event. Always have an escape route—a reason to leave and a form of transportation to get home in, like an Uber or cab. Keep sober people's numbers in your phone in case you need to text or call them for a pep talk. Eat food before going. Take mints or gum so you can change the taste in your mouth should you start craving alcohol. Get a water, diet soda, or iced tea in your hand immediately, because often the host just wants to be polite, not push you to get drunk, and other patrons may not want to feel like they're drinking alone.

Remember this mantra: "For right now, I am not going to drink." Leave early too. No one is paying that much attention to your presence anyway. In this day of flakiness, they're probably happy you showed up at all—plus we know you've shut down enough parties back in your using days. Then, most importantly: revel in being hangover-free the next day!

You also have to be okay knowing that sometimes your sobriety will make people uncomfortable. For example, my fiancé Jim and I were at a big house party sitting in the hot tub when the host got in and said he felt bad that he was fucked up in front of us. When I asked why, he said he thought we wished we were drinking and doing drugs too. I responded: "OMG, I absolutely do not want to be doing either, and I'm having a blast watching the cool ambiance (there were Cirque du Soleil performers swinging over our heads) and I can't wait to get up tomorrow morning not hung-over and work out!" I left out the part about how I'd just hooked up with Jim in a room in the host's mega-mansion. (See? I can still be scandalous in sobriety!)

This was part of the reason I threw a charity event in 2017 called Sexy Sober Sunday which raised $10,000 for the addiction non-profit organization Shatterproof. It was a delicious brunch at a nice beach hotel where no alcohol was served, just fancy mocktails. Over 100 guests dressed up in cocktail attire and got their picture taken on a red carpet. There was a DJ playing hip hop music and the dance floor was packed. Most of the people who came to support me were not sober and told me afterwards how surprised they were to have had so much fun without drinking.

My mission for Sexy Sober Sunday was just that: to prove that you can have fun and dance and be glamorous without a glass of champagne in your hand! I also wanted to show that people who recover from their addictions and get their lives back on track should be celebrated and congratulated for being strong enough to beat this disease. We are not all like the sober characters on TV and in movies who constantly relapse as part of the plotline. And if you have a friend who's struggling with drinking, one of the best ways to support them is to offer to do an activity with them that doesn't involve alcohol.

If you're reading this book and debating getting sober or trying to do it, I leave you with this advice from a TedX talk I watched by motivational speaker and author Mel Robbins called "How to Stop Screwing Yourself Over." Mel says that in any area of your life you want to change, one fact will always come into play: "You are never going to feel like it!" People who go on diets don't want to eat healthy all the time;

the same goes for those who have to drag themselves to the gym nonstop to lose weight. Nobody *wants* to get sober or stop using their drug of choice! I certainly didn't. But there comes a time when you just have to grow up and do the right thing before you ruin your career or marriage, go to jail, end up in a mental institution, hurt someone else or even die.

Mel recommends experimenting with the five second rule, which means if you have an impulse, you must marry it with an action within five seconds. If you don't, you kill the idea and it won't happen. She says scientists call this sort of thing "activation energy," which is the force required to get you to do something new and change what you are currently doing on autopilot. If you want to explore new ways to have fun being sober, remember the five second rule and book that trip, sign up for that class, get off your ass and take a walk or go meditate. You will become a more evolved, interesting person this way by building different life experiences aside from simply partying. The reverse works too: if you're craving a drink, refrain from getting one for just five seconds and let the idea pass. Just keep doing this over and over again and you will build your sober time one day at a time.

Finally, don't forget that you control the message about your sobriety, and no one can take that away from you. I go back to *The Fifth Agreement* by Don Miguel Ruiz. His first agreement is "Be Impeccable with Your Word." You are the messenger. Your happiness is up to you, so tell a beautiful story about yourself. For example: I love being sober and am a badass for living life on life's terms and getting through tough shit that most people would have to numb out to deal with.

Our minds are so powerful that they perceive the stories we create. So don't talk badly about yourself, like saying sobriety sucks or you're bored and depressed. Never betray yourself or gossip about others—who cares if someone thinks you'll relapse or are a drag sober? Life is a dream. Our minds are always dreaming, and when we become aware of that, it gives us the key to change the dream if we're not enjoying it.

I choose to believe that being in recovery is empowering. I'm not a quitter, or weak, or a risk to hire. I'm an asset. I live a beautiful substance-free life and have tons of fun, meaningful experiences and connections. It's the best life decision I've ever made. You'll never know the rewards unless you give sobriety a try. If you're struggling with the process, keep hanging in there and wait for the miracle. It's totally worth it, I promise.

Friel The Love: being supported by my KTLA co-workers at Sexy Sober Sunday

Walking like an Egyptian on a camel in front of the Pyramids of Giza

ACKNOWLEDGMENTS

You have no idea how much gratitude I have for Anna David and Launch Pad Publishing for believing in this book and physically bringing it into the world.

Thank you to Debra Ollivier for giving me the inspiration, structure, and guidance to get the "Pretty Sobering News" process started.

As for my book cover: credit for the fabulous makeup job (complete with fake cuts and bruises) goes to Chanty Lagrana, and to Bob Marshall for shooting the pictures and merging them together. Thank you to Onur Aksoy for taking their work and making it into the amazing cover.

For my son, Cash, and daughter, Cameron, thank you for choosing me to be your mom. I love you with all my heart. You make me a better person and help me to stay sober every day.

To my future husband, Jim Hecht: you're my spiritual/ sober soulmate, my meditation/yoga partner, and my best friend who cracks me up. Thank you for being my cheer-leader, and I can't wait to spend the rest of my life with you.

Much appreciation for my KTLA 5 News Director Jason Ball for supporting my sobriety by allowing me to write this book, and also for greenlighting my sober video podcast "Keepin' It Friel: Conversations on Recovery" (which you can check out on ktla.com or iTunes, hint hint).

Finally, thanks to my parents, sisters, friends, co-workers, and fans for accepting and encouraging this sober journey I'm on. I'm so grateful and blessed.

Made in the USA
Las Vegas, NV
05 May 2024

89570989R00069